Ending Life Issues

Ending Life Issues

Six Essays on Abortion and Euthanasia

CHRIS CHRISTIANSEN

WIPF & STOCK · Eugene, Oregon

ENDING LIFE ISSUES
Six Essays on Abortion and Euthanasia

Wipf & Stock
An Imprint of Wipf and Stock Publishers
199 W. 8th Ave., Suite 3
Eugene, OR 97401

www.wipfandstock.com

PAPERBACK ISBN: 979-8-3852-5991-5
HARDCOVER ISBN: 979-8-3852-5992-2
EBOOK ISBN: 979-8-3852-5993-9

03/03/26

This book is dedicated to my grandma, Rachel Herrmann, the first nurse I ever met, who still talks about her love for her patients to this day.

Contents

Acknowledgments

I WOULD LIKE TO begin by thanking my Lord and Savior Jesus Christ. I believe that he has given me a passion for these subjects and I am blessed that I get to work for his kingdom, defending the lives of people at the beginning and end of their lives. Thank you, mom and dad, for pushing me to go to school in the first place. It opened up opportunities such as this. Thank you to my wife, Amy, for her constant support and pushing me to finally get a book written. Thank you to Paul Chamberlain, my professor and good friend, who is always there to bounce some ideas off of. Thank you to the Human Defense Initiative for giving me my start, writing articles on these topics. Thank you to Hendrik van der Breggen, who read this manuscript in its very rough draft and gave numerous suggestions to help make it a better book. Thank you to FVASH (Fraser Valley Atheists, Skeptics, and Humanists), who let me be part of their group for five years and taught me how to defend my beliefs. Thank you to my friends Nick, Alex, Zeke, Zac, and countless others, who supported and kept me sane through this process. Finally, I would like to thank Ben and Anjelika, Dan, Sheldon and Robyn, Lando, Collin, and many others who contributed to my GoFundMe to help this project be completed.

Introduction

This is not a book you have to read from cover to cover. Rather, it is a collection of essays on topics I've had ideas about for a while. You can read them all, or you can read one. You won't hurt my feelings if you skip a couple because I won't know. (Unless you're a friend or family member. Then I expect you to read every single essay and like it!)

My first essay, "Does Paul Chamberlain Dream of T-Rexes and Electrified Fences?" is really about showing that people have concerns about slippery slopes for good reasons. Paul Chamberlain, a Canadian philosopher, made a prediction about what would happen if euthanasia were legalized and the impact it would have on people. I will show how his prediction came to pass.

I was inspired to write my second essay, "Lessons from a Birmingham Jail," by Martin Luther King Jr.'s famous letter, which I had read for a master's class. Many of the points he made seem to carry over into the struggle to end abortion. My hope is that this essay will shake people out of complacency and also encourage those who are fighting the good fight.

My third essay, "Going All the Way (to Infanticide)," is a Socratic dialogue. The plot revolves around a woman who is considering whether to let her baby die because he has Down's syndrome, a hospital chaplain who is trying to convince her to choose life, and a Canaanite storm god who wants the baby dead.

My fourth essay, "A Brainless Suggestion," is an argumentative essay about why it is immoral to engineer brainless human beings so that we can harvest their organs.

My fifth essay, "An Out-of-This-World Problem," is an ethical case study. It involves a fictional scenario where aliens have crash-landed on earth and are dying of a horrible disease. It seeks to provide a framework for deciding whether they should be given medical assistance in dying.

My last essay is a book review. This will likely be the most academic essay of the six. I've read two books by David Boonin called *A Defense of Abortion* and *Beyond Roe.* He is a major thinker in the pro-choice movement that abortion opponents should be aware of.

I hope these essays are informative, alarming, and challenging. And most of all, I hope they will be a tool that others can use to further the cause of life.

Chris Christiansen, 2023

Essay 1

Does Paul Chamberlain Dream of T-Rexes and Electrified Fences?

One of my favorite movies is *Jurassic Park*. One of the most terrifying moments in the movie is when the power in the park goes out, and the Tyrannosaurus Rex breaks free. The character Ian Malcolm, a chaos theoretician, had been predicting throughout the entire movie that a park trying to control extinct creatures would never work. No one seemed to take him seriously until that moment. And, as he watches the Rex gain its freedom, he wryly utters to himself, "Boy, do I hate being right all the time."[1]

I have seen someone else make predictions that came to pass. He hadn't been to an amusement park with dinosaurs in it. Instead, Canadian philosopher Paul Chamberlain saw people pushing for Physician Assisted Suicide (from here on, PAS) to be legalized in Canada. And he predicted it would have devastating results. I don't know what response he received personally, but when, years ago, I used his arguments in conversations, they were often dismissed as alarmist. Now, it seems, he was right to be worried.

In this essay, I am going to lay out a couple of the arguments that Chamberlain made, and then show the trajectory that the legalization of PAS has traveled on in Canada. (It's "Medical Assistance in Dying" now [MAID]. However, I refuse to use a sanitized

1. Spielberg, *Jurassic Park*.

title that avoids owning up to the fact that we are telling people suicide is a good thing.) My thesis is that the slippery slope is as steep—and slippery—as Chamberlain thought.

The Lowering of Safe Guards

Chamberlain imagined that safe guards would originally be put in place to protect certain groups of people: "The person must be terminally ill. There must be a written request. Two physicians need to be involved, and the request for suicide must be persistent over a period of time."[2] Chamberlain replies, however, that

> the argument against legalizing PAS is that it is a practice that, if made legal, would be difficult, maybe impossible, to contain. Legalizing this practice today would lead to practices we all agree would be wrong and unfortunate, such as PAS for teenagers and for people who are not even terminally ill but just emotionally depressed, people being euthanized with no request, and infanticide.[3]

I want to draw attention to his point about euthanizing people who are emotionally depressed. As evidence that this is an inevitable outcome, he points to the true story of a fifty-year-old woman in the Netherlands, who was mentally depressed instead of physically ill. She had an abusive alcoholic husband, and her two sons had died, one by suicide. Tragically, even though it wasn't legal at the time, she asked for PAS and her doctor gave it to her. The doctor was taken to court for this illegal action but was exonerated. Chamberlain believed at the time that a similar loosening of restrictions would happen in Canada.[4] So, what did end up happening?

2. Chamberlain, *Final Wishes*, 86.
3. Chamberlain, "Case Against Physician Assisted Suicide," para. 33.
4. Chamberlain, *Final Wishes*, 120.

History of PAS in Canada So Far

In 2015, the Supreme Court of Canada ruled that "people with grievous and irremediable medical conditions should have the right to ask a doctor to help them die."[5]

And as predicted, safeguards were put in place. However, fast forward just seven years, and changes are already being made. The College of Pharmacists of British Columbia state,

> While the patient must still have a "grievous and irremediable medical condition," a reasonably foreseeable natural death is no longer a requirement for MAiD eligibility. However, patients whose sole underlying condition is mental illness will not be eligible at this time. *Note: In two years, this restriction will be removed. However, the Act requires that an independent review determine recommended protocols, guidance and safeguards to apply to requests made for medical assistance in dying by persons who have a mental illness.*[6]

Keep in mind, when Chamberlain made his argument, it was in the year 2000, a decade and a half before PAS was legalized, and a little over two decades before the safe guards are to be lowered. (Canada has since postponed the decision until 2027. However, the fact remains that this is still something they want to go ahead with.)

Analysis of the Trend

Did Chamberlain have some preternatural power that helped him see this outcome? In a sense. He used the power of logic. More specifically, he followed the logic of the pro-euthanasia argument where it naturally leads. The fundamental principle that the legalization of PAS rests on is the right to choose to end your suffering on your own terms. People may say this only applies to those who

5. Peyton, "Supreme Court Says Yes," para. 1.

6. College of Pharmacists of British Columbia, "New Federal Legislation Brings Changes," paras. 9–12.

are physically suffering, but who are we to say that someone suffering from depression is not suffering as badly as a terminal cancer patient? And who are we to interfere with a depressed person's personal autonomy?[7]

Chamberlain is not saying that wandering down the slippery slope was the intent of all the parties responsible for legalizing PAS. Rather, he was raising awareness that

> sometimes one action does more than simply *invite* the question of pursuing the next action. There are times when the reasons we set out for doing one thing actually *justify* other actions that we have not yet begun to pursue and may not even be thinking of at the time.[8]

There was also an unintended consequence that he was right about.

The Increased Burden

I want to get personal for a moment. I have a very large phobia of doctors. When I think about getting a check-up or physical exam, it is enough to make me go catatonic. It's not so much that I am afraid of finding out I'm sick. I'm not even afraid of dying. I am afraid of all the procedures that I'd have to endure to get better. Of course, the catch-22 is that if I don't get the treatment, I worry that I'll die in excruciating agony anyway.

As a Christian, I don't believe that suicide is ever the right choice. Now, I can hear proponents of PAS saying, "Well, if you don't like euthanasia, don't get euthanized." But that's not the point. Before, PAS was not an option, so by default, I could never ask a doctor to do it because it was not legal. Now, if I am ever in that situation, there will always be a temptation to take it. I worry that I might give into it. And, phobia or no phobia, I suspect I'm not alone in thinking this.[9]

7. Chamberlain, "Case Against Physician Assisted Suicide," paras. 23–24.
8. Chamberlain, *Final Wishes*, 112.
9. Thanks to Hendrik van der Breggen for suggesting this particular line.

And this puts the lie to the characterization of PAS as a purely private decision between a patient and their doctor. The legalization of it was a public policy change that Chamberlain predicted would put more pressure on people who are already vulnerable.[10]

Conclusion

Chamberlain made other predictions that I see as having the potential to come true. I will be watching the news for future developments with great interest (and trepidation). And while I hope and pray it doesn't go further than what I've laid out, the general lack of respect for human life that I see growing in our culture doesn't leave me feeling optimistic.

So, I wonder, as Paul Chamberlain watches these events unfold, if he, like Ian Malcolm, thinks to himself, "Boy, do I hate being right all the time."

10. Chamberlain, "Case Against Physician Assisted Suicide," para. 14.

Essay 2

Lessons from a Birmingham Jail

Martin Luther King Jr.'s "Letter from a Birmingham Jail" was written, according to Jonathan Wolff, while King "was held in jail after being arrested for taking part in a political protest for racial equality in Alabama."[1] In this letter, King calls Christian clergymen to stop being complacent and join the fight against racism.

This letter is full of practical advice for how to resist social injustice in society, and while King was talking about racism, I believe that many of the points he makes apply to Christians who are wondering if we should oppose abortion. The point of this essay is to demonstrate those applications.

You're Asking for Trouble!

King begins his letter by stating that

> injustice anywhere is a threat to justice everywhere. We are caught in an inescapable network of mutuality, tied in a single garment of destiny. Whatever affects one directly, affects all indirectly.[2]

The injustice that King had in mind was discrimination against him and other African Americans based on the color of

1. Wolff, *Readings in Moral*, 512.
2. King, "Letter from a Birmingham Jail," 522.

their skin. He understood that discrimination of any kind will beget more discrimination.

The injustice of discrimination is being carried out against the unborn as well via abortion. Pro-choicers are saying that being human is not enough to qualify for human rights. You must be human plus something else. For Richard Dawkins, size seems to be the relevant feature: "A certain kind of religious mind cannot see the moral difference between killing a microscopic cluster of cells on the one hand, and killing a fully-grown doctor on the other."[3] So, unborn human beings are being discriminated against here based on their size.

How could this lead to injustice for others? Well, apparently, according to Dawkins, you have to be about the same size as a doctor before you have a right not to be killed. But, if applied consistently, that would make it okay to kill newborn infants, toddlers, young children, and even some teenagers, and adults. Basically, as Scott Klusendorf writes,

> If humans only have value because of some acquired property . . . and not in virtue of the kind of thing they are, then it follows that since these acquired properties come in varying degrees, basic human rights come in varying degrees. . . . This relegates the proposition that all men are created equal to the ash heap of history.[4]

This is a good warning against complacency. Of course, even if we were never impacted directly by such discrimination, it is still something that Christians should be fighting against. As John G. Stackhouse writes, "Christians provide a service, increasing *shalom*, when we stand up against any oppression, including intellectual and cultural oppression, and particularly on behalf of the weak—in this case, children."[5]

3. Dawkins, *God Delusion*, 333.

4. Klusendorf, *Case for Life*, 53. They have other criteria as well, such as whether they are conscious, viable, or able to survive on their own. Chapters 2–3 of Klusendorf's book have some helpful responses to these criteria.

5. Stackhouse, *Making the Best of It*, 334.

Be Prepared!

King says that there are three steps for launching a nonviolent campaign, the first of which is a "collection of the facts to determine whether injustices exist."[6] During his time, these injustices included racial segregation, brutality, unjust treatment in the courts, and the unsolved bombings of African American homes and churches.[7]

What sort of facts can we collect to show that injustices are occurring against the unborn? Well, as I already pointed out, they are being discriminated against by being denied human rights. In its preamble, the United Nations Declaration of Human Rights says, "Whereas recognition of the inherent dignity and of the equal and inalienable rights of all members of the human family is the foundation of freedom, justice and peace in the world."[8] The unborn are members of the human family, so their inherent dignity and inalienable rights should be recognized. The Declaration further warns, "Whereas disregard and contempt for human rights have resulted in barbarous acts which have outraged the conscience of mankind."[9] What sort of barbarous acts has the discrimination against the unborn led to?

Simply, they are not being looked after by their parents to such an extent that they are being deliberately killed. As Klusendorf argues, "We . . . have a duty to sustain our own offspring."[10] And, as the United Nations Convention on the Rights of the Child states, "The child, by reason of his physical and mental immaturity, needs special safeguards and care, including appropriate legal protection, before as well as after birth."[11] While reading this, I can't escape the distressing implication that Canada, by virtue of allowing abortion to remain legal, is guilty of human rights violations.

6. King, "Letter from a Birmingham Jail," 522.
7. King, "Letters from a Birmingham Jail," 522.
8. United Nations, "Universal Declaration of Human Rights," para. 1.
9. United Nations, "Universal Declaration of Human Rights," para. 2.
10. Klusendorf, *Case for Life*, 188.
11. United Nations, "Convention on the Rights," para. 10.

After all, Canada was one of the countries that signed that human rights statement.

Instead of having the parents look after their children, countries that allow abortion are letting the children be killed through brutal methods. John Jefferson Davis describes some of the most common abortion procedures. First, there is vacuum curettage where the cervix is dilated, and a suction device is inserted into the uterus, which tears the baby apart. The doctors then assemble all the pieces to make sure nothing is left inside. The second is dilation and curettage. The cervix is dilated and the baby is cut to pieces, then the uterine wall is scraped clean. The third is dilation and evacuation, which is used during the thirteenth to sixteenth weeks of gestation. The baby has developed more of a skeleton and skull at this time, so those bones must first be crushed before the doctor can remove the baby with a suction device. The fourth is a hysterotomy. During this procedure, an incision is made in the abdomen and the baby is pulled out, then left to die. The fifth is chemical abortions. Here, substances are sometimes used to induce a miscarriage. The sixth is a saline abortion. The doctor will inject a saline solution into the amniotic sac. The baby breathes it in and is poisoned as a result.[12] If I heard about this happening to any born human being, I would consider it a grave injustice. Since I view the unborn as human beings of equal worth and value to the rest of us, I also view these abortion procedures as an injustice.

I would argue that there is an injustice being done to women as well. They are being promised that abortion is a safe medical procedure that can spare them future difficulties caused by an unwanted pregnancy. However, there are many physical and mental health issues that arise from abortion. On the Silent No More Campaign website, women share their testimonies about the impact that abortion has had on them. Kathryn from Ohio describes her physical health complications:

> Heavy bleeding went on for weeks and the clinic would not help. . . . I believe I was also sterilized. I later developed painful adenomyosis—where scar tissue traps

12. Davis, *Evangelical Ethics*, 143–44.

> endometrial tissue. My only cause: uterine scarring from abortion. Because of this I later underwent a full hysterectomy.[13]

Meanwhile, Sue writes about her emotional pain.

> I was very depressed. I had low self-esteem. I became an emotional eater and gained lots of weight. I became very promiscuous. . . . I suffered from severe depression, guilt and regret that were overwhelming. . . . All these problems were more than likely consequences of the abortion.[14]

Abortion does not seem to be able to deliver on its promises. Silent No More is full of testimonies from women who, by having an abortion, have suffered the very difficulties they were trying to avoid. As a result, women are paying the price for the misinformation.

Be Ready for Persecution

King writes,

> Mindful of the difficulties involved, we decided to undertake a process of self-purification. We began a series of workshops on nonviolence, and we repeatedly asked ourselves "Are you able to accept blows without retaliating?" "Are you able to endure the ordeal of jail?"[15]

King's group was entering a battlefield, and these were important questions for them to be asking themselves.

The situation is no different for pro-life advocates. I have seen videos of pro-choicers being verbally abusive.[16] Ask yourself if you are ready to respond with humility and love. I saw another video where a pro-choice man kicked a video camera out of a woman's

13. Kathryn, "Loved too Late," para. 4.
14. Sue, "Sue's 2023 March for Life," para. 4.
15. King, "Letter from a Birmingham Jail," 647.
16. WSYX ABC 6, "Caught on Camera," 0:05.

hand.[17] Ask yourself if you're ready to not punch or kick back. I watched a video where a young girl walked by a pro-life booth and stole the pro-lifers' sign. A police officer had to chase her down and arrest her for theft.[18] Ask yourself if you're willing to not resort to the same cheap methods against pro-choice displays. Finally, I've heard stories of pro-lifers being arrested when they've blocked abortion clinics. Ask yourself if you could you handle the consequences of civil disobedience?

Basically, we need to ask ourselves if we are ready to behave like the man who founded our faith: Jesus Christ. As Paul Chamberlain writes, "Jesus did no violence to anyone. He was on the receiving end of plenty of violence, but he was never the source of it."[19]

Once you've gotten yourself familiarized with the facts and you know you're ready for the pushback, take King's third step: "direct action."[20]

Don't Be Afraid to Use Unpopular Methods

One of the pushbacks that King received was that other clergy felt he should have tried to negotiate with the leaders of Birmingham rather than protest. King's response was to inform them that he had tried negotiating. He had received promises from the leaders that they would take steps to end the discrimination. Those promises were never kept.[21] You can almost feel King's frustration as he writes these words:

> As in so many past experiences, our hopes had been blasted, and the shadow of deep disappointment settled upon us. We had no alternative except to prepare for direct action, whereby we would present our very bodies as

17. Toronto Sun, "Caught on Camera," 0:26–0:27,
18. Darth Yucko, "She Stole His Sign," 0:20–3:42.
19. Chamberlain, *Why People Don't* Believe, 116.
20. King, "Letter from a Birmingham Jail," 522.
21. King, "Letter from a Birmingham Jail," 522.

> a means of laying our case before the conscience of the local and national community.[22]

Pro-lifers have done similar things like blocking abortion clinics by standing outside of them. Sometimes, like King and his group, they even went to jail for it.

But another form of unpopular method that we should be willing to use is abortion images. These are pictures of what unborn babies look like after the abortion procedure has been done. In his studies of social movements, Jonathon Van Maren observes that "powerful photographs have changed public opinion, and altered the course of history as a result."[23]

You might think that this goes against what I said earlier about not doing different kinds of violence to people. After all, if a woman who has had an abortion sees those images, it might cause her psychological pain and guilt. However, Van Maren makes an important point here.

> Abortion hurts women *because* abortion kills children. Nearly half of women who have abortions have already had at least one previous abortion. Post-abortive women are very often also *pre-abortive* women. Post-abortive women are one of our main target audiences, considering the very high risk that they will abort again. It is our goal to reach women who have had abortions with the truth so that the truth can save the lives of other children.[24]

It is not unjust violence to confront someone with the reality of the wrong that they have done.

Ignore People Who Tell You to Wait

King was told by the clergymen to wait for things to change on their own. His reply is a good reminder of the folly of such a suggestion.

22. King, "Letter from a Birmingham Jail," 522.
23. Van Maren, *Seeing Is Believing*, 38.
24. Van Maren, *Seeing Is Believing*, 90.

> We know through painful experience that freedom is never voluntarily given by the oppressor; it must be demanded by the oppressed. Frankly, I have yet to engage in a direct-action campaign that was "well timed" in the view of those who have not suffered unduly from the disease of segregation. For years now I have heard the word "Wait!" It rings in the ear of every Negro with piercing familiarity. This "Wait" has almost always meant "Never." We must come to see, with one of our distinguished jurists, that "justice too long delayed is justice denied."[25]

I am going to make two predictions. First, I predict that the right to life is not going to be granted willingly by women who believe that it is their right to have an abortion. And it is not going to be willingly granted by the abortion industry that is making bank off of killing unborn children.

My second prediction is that the unborn are not ever going to be able to demand their right to life from their oppressors. Sadly, they just can't think or talk at this point. So, as long as there are helpless people who can't stand up for themselves, there needs to be people who are willing to stand in the gap for them.

Pro-choicers are constantly telling us to wait. They want us to wait for more birth control and sex education to be available. They want us to wait until many of the social ills that cause women to want abortions have been solved. Some even have suggested waiting for the pro-life side to have a better public image. I get the distinct impression that they also want it to be the case that the unborn are never granted the right to life.

In the meantime, justice is being denied to the unborn. Christians wouldn't wait if born children were being torn apart or poisoned by their parents. Since the unborn are of equal value to born children, why should we wait while the same things are done to them?

25. King, "Letter from a Birmingham Jail," 523.

Conclusion

There are many lessons for the pro-life movement in King's letter: injustice leads to more injustice. Be prepared with the relevant facts about the injustices that are occurring. Be ready for opposition. Don't shy away from using unpopular methods. Most importantly, act. Throughout all of this, pro-life education is very important. I encourage you to read King's letter for yourself and find your own lessons. As you do, remember the tools John Newport says God has given his church to empower us: "Power in the cross and resurrection and the coming of the Holy Spirit."[26] Only they can bring true change to minds and hearts.

26. Newport, *New Age Movement*, 531.

Essay 3

Going All the Way (to Infanticide)

SARAH WALKED DOWN THE hall of the hospital in a daze. Her eyes stared straight ahead, not really seeing the patients or staff around her. Sensing that she was in deep pain, everyone gave her a wide berth.

How could this happen? she thought to herself. *We did all the tests. They said he was perfectly healthy. If I had known, I would have dealt with this much earlier. I don't want to give him up to a stranger. But I'm not ready for this kind of burden. Derek doesn't want it either.*

These thoughts kept playing on repeat in her mind. Finally, the dam broke. She leaned against the wall and started crying. The sobs came from deep within her. It hurt, but at the same time, it was therapeutic to release all the pent-up emotions she had been holding in since the day before.

When the sobs finally subsided, she felt a little more with it. However, the problem had not gone away. She just wished she had someone she could talk to who was not as emotionally invested in the situation.

When she looked up, she realized she was standing in front of the hospital chapel. She couldn't help but smirk. *If I actually believed in God, I would think he orchestrated this*, she thought. *Oh well, any port in a storm.*

She pushed open the door. There were about twenty chairs facing the front. The walls were painted a soothing blue. At the front of the room was a podium. Behind it, a cross hung on the wall. A young man was reading a Bible.

Sarah walked in, closed the door softly behind her, then headed to the front. "Excuse me, are you the chaplain?" she asked.

The young man looked up. He was in his thirties with short brown hair, blue eyes, and a baby face. "Yes, I am. My name is Chris."

"Sarah," she smiled tightly and extended her hand.

"Are you looking for prayer?" Chris asked.

"No. I'm not a believer. But I was looking for some advice."

"Well, I will try and help any way I can. Have a seat." Chris gestured to a chair.

Once they were seated, Sarah took a few minutes to gather her thoughts, then launched into the story. "A couple of days ago, I had a baby. His name is Ian."

"Congratulations. That's wonderful," Chris smiled.

"My husband Derek and I thought so, too," Sarah sighed.

Chris grew more somber. "What changed?"

"We did amniocentesis. All of the tests came back negative. But when he was born, we found out the tests didn't work. He has Down's syndrome."

"That's tough."

"And that's not all. He was born with an incomplete esophagus."

"That's a common problem with Down's syndrome babies."

"I know."

"But it's also completely treatable. The doctors can do surgery to reconstruct the passage from the mouth to the stomach."

"I know that, too. The doctor walked us through it."

Chris wanted to ask her what the problem was then, but he sensed she needed to come out and say it on her own.

Finally, she said, "But neither Derek nor I want to raise a child with Down's syndrome."

Chris kept his expression neutral. "So, you're thinking about giving him up for adoption?"

"No. The thought of giving him to a stranger terrifies me. Who knows what sort of life he would have? What our doctor has suggested is that we keep him comfortable but not feed him intravenously."

"The doctor is suggesting that you let him die?"[1]

"Yes. And I mean, it makes sense to me. He's not going to have a great quality of life. We'd be saving him from suffering. But on the other hand . . ."

"He's still your son."

"Exactly." Even though Sarah thought she had cried all that she could, the tears started flowing again. "I'm bonded with him. I don't know what to do."

Chris quietly prayed for a moment. *Lord, I don't want to scare this woman off. But I also don't want her baby to die. Help me to be gracious and loving while speaking the truth. I leave the results in your hands. Amen.*

A quiet voice said to him, *Be honest.*

Chris opened his hands. "I should tell you up front that I am on the pro-life side of things."

Sarah gave a sad smile. "I sort of expected that from a chaplain."

"Would you be okay with me sharing some reasons for why I think you should let your son live?"

Sarah nodded. "Any advice is welcome right now."

Suddenly, there was a crash of thunder. Both Sarah and Chris looked up at the ceiling of the chapel. A seven-foot-tall man with a long beard was floating there. He wore a helmet with two horns protruding from it. In his right hand, he carried a mace. In his left hand, he carried a lightning bolt. "Who the heck is that?" Sarah asked.

1. This whole scenario is based on the case of Baby Doe. Warnock and MacDonald write about it in *Easeful Death*, 36.

Before Chris could answer, the man started speaking in a snooty voice. "Not so fast. Behold, it is I, Baal. Canaanite god of the storm. And I am here to stop you from guilting this woman into doing something she doesn't want to do."[2]

Sarah became indignant. "I am perfectly capable of thinking for myself on this issue."

Baal smiled at her like an indulgent parent. "Of course you are, dear. I'm sure you would not object to an open discussion?"

Chris gestured at Sarah. "It's really up to her. It's her life that we are discussing."

Sarah looked between them. "Are we really just accepting that a pagan storm god is hanging out on your ceiling? Yes? . . . Okay." She took a deep breath. "Yeah, I'd be willing to listen to what you both have to say."

Who Gets Human Rights?

Chris and Sarah sat side by side facing Baal. Baal began to float back and forth, as if pacing. "Sarah, you said that you and your husband are pro-choice. Why do you believe that abortion is morally acceptable?"

"I guess, we hold to the same view as Mary Anne Warren," Sarah replied. "We acknowledge that the unborn baby is biologically human, but we don't think that is enough to give him a right to life. He must also be a person."[3]

"Very good," Baal nodded. "You and I are in agreement so far. And what do you believe makes someone a person?"

"The traits that Warren listed seem reasonable: consciousness, reasoning ability, self-motivated activity, the ability to communicate, and self-awareness. Like her, I don't think you need to possess all of these traits. But consciousness is an important

2. The idea for a dialogue between a Christian and a pagan god comes from the LutheranSatire videos about Horus. LutheranSatire, "Horus Reads the Internet."

3. Warren, "On the Moral and Legal," 345.

starting point, and that combined with reasoning and self motivated activity seem sufficient to me for personhood."[4]

"Overall, we agree. May I suggest, then, that you have all the justification you need for ending the life of your son?"

"Walk me through it."

"It's quite simple, really," replied Baal. "As Peter Singer argues, the arguments that show an unborn baby is not a person with a right to life apply to the newborn baby as much as to the fetus. 'A week-old baby is not a rational and self-aware being. . . . If . . . the fetus . . . does not have the same claim to life as a person, it appears that the newborn baby does not either.'[5] Now Sarah, you would have aborted it if you had known it had Down's syndrome, right?"

Sarah nodded. "Yes."

"And that's because he was not a person with a right to life?"

"Agreed."

"Well, since he is still not a person with a right to life by your standard, what is the problem with letting him die now?"

Sarah digested that. "Okay, Chris do you have anything to say to that?"

"Quite a few things," Chris replied, as he leaned forward. "First, I noticed a glaring weakness in your argument, Baal. Your case for infanticide seems to rest on the foundation of your arguments for abortion. That means that if the argument for abortion fails, then the argument for infanticide would fall like a house of cards, too."

"Good thing it is air tight then!" smiled Baal.

"Actually, one of the first things you said was factually incorrect, at least according to our human rights documents. You claimed that it is not enough for Ian to be a human being. He also had to be a person before he is given human rights, correct?"

"True."

"Okay, now let's look at what the Universal Declaration of Human Rights has to say. In the preamble, it states the following: 'Whereas recognition of the inherent dignity and of the equal and

4. Warren, "On the Moral and Legal," 346.

5. Singer, *Practical Ethics*, loc. 151.

inalienable rights of all members of the human family is the foundation of freedom, justice and peace in the world.'"[6] Chris turned to Sarah. "You and your husband are both human, correct?"

Sarah laughed. "Last time I checked."

"That tells me something important. If both parents are human, then, as Stephanie Gray writes, 'Wouldn't it follow that their offspring must be human?'[7] I mean you didn't give birth to a whale, right?"

"It felt like it in the moment, but yes, it's true. Ian is human."

"Is he growing?"

Sarah whistled. "Is he ever. I swear he's going to have outgrown all the outfits that I bought for him by next month."

"Good to know. That leads to Gray's next question. If he is growing, wouldn't it follow that he is alive?"[8]

"Sure."

"So, since Ian is a living member of the human family, that means he has the same inherent value that the rest of us have, and therefore, he should have the same rights as us. And, according to Section 3 of UDHR, that includes the inalienable right to life."[9]

"So, you're saying that personhood does not factor into human rights at all?" Sarah asked.

"No, it does. I'm saying that if a living human is present, then a person is present. In section 6, it says quite clearly that 'everyone has the right to recognition everywhere as a person before the law.'[10] I think the reference of 'everyone' includes any and all members of the human family."

"That's a lot to digest. Can we grab some coffee from the vending machine while I mull it over?" asked Sarah.

"Sounds good to me. All this talking makes my throat dry," said Chris.

Baal sighed, "Human needs really slow down the process."

6. United Nations, "Universal Declaration of Human Rights," para. 1.

7. Gray, *Love Unleashes Life*, 35.

8. Gray, *Love Unleashes Life*, 35.

9. United Nations, "Universal Declaration of Human Rights," para. 13.

10. United Nations, "Universal Declaration of Human Rights," para. 16.

It's Not Rational!

A few minutes later, Sarah and Chris had their coffees and were sitting down again.

Sarah asked, "So, Chris, why do you feel like it's so important that we grant the personhood of all humans?"

"Probably for the same reason that the people who composed the UDHR felt that way. I want to avoid human rights abuses," Chris replied. "The UDHR was created in the aftermath of World War II. The Holocaust was probably fresh in their minds. They had seen the atrocities done by the Nazi government against the Jewish people. As one scholar David G. Thompson put it, 'In the harrowing aftermath of the war, the international community came to a critical juncture where abuse of citizens by governments was so reprehensible that all nations agreed, at least in word, on the necessity of international prohibitions against atrocities.'[11] That's why the UDHR even says in the preamble, 'Whereas disregard and contempt for human rights have resulted in barbarous acts which have outraged the conscience of mankind.'"[12]

"So, you are basically accusing pro-choicers of human rights violations?" Sarah asked a little offended.

"Actually, I'm claiming that any country that signed this charter but still allows abortions is guilty of human rights violations," Chris replied. "Especially when they also created what's called the Convention of the Rights of the Child, which says in the preamble, 'The child, by reason of his physical and mental immaturity, needs special safeguards and care, including appropriate legal protection, before as well as after birth.'[13] The irony is that the very traits that this document says make Ian worthy of protection are the basis for why you and Baal think it's justified to kill him."

"I guess I could reject the authority of those documents," Sarah pointed out.

11. Thompson, "High Price of Unity," 101.

12. United Nations, "Universal Declaration of Human Rights," para. 2.

13. United Nations, "Convention on the Rights," para. 10.

"Yes. I've considered that, too. Maybe one day, we'll rewrite them and say being a human isn't enough. But then, I don't think we've learned anything from World War II at all. For that matter, I don't think we've learned anything from human history. As Catholic apologist Trent Horn writes, 'Every time in history a group of human beings has been disqualified from being considered people (e.g., blacks, women, Jews, the mentally handicapped), the reason for the disqualification turned out to be bogus.'"[14]

"Okay, I think I've heard enough," Baal interjected. "You can't seriously believe that a newborn baby is capable of exercising rationality, do you?"

"No, but I believe that they have a basic root capacity for it. I'll get to that later. But along with our human rights documents, I think the child's abilities are irrelevant. The UN Convention of the Rights of the Child says, 'States Parties shall respect and ensure the rights set forth in the present Convention to each child within their jurisdiction without discrimination of any kind.'[15] You, Baal, my friend, are advocating for discriminating against children based on age."

"That is a straw man!" Baal snapped. "I am saying they are not persons based on their lack of rationality. I am not discriminating based on their age."

"Oh, really. Along with Gray, I'd like to ask you why a newborn baby is not rational?"

"It's brain has not developed enough yet."

"Why has it not developed enough yet?"

"It hasn't had time."

"Okay," Chris continued, "So, once again, we know something important about the unborn. They are not rational because their brain hasn't developed enough yet. And their brain hasn't developed enough yet because they haven't had time.[16] And, as Gray

14. Horn, *Persuasive Pro-Life*, 128.

15. United Nations, "Convention on the Rights," para. 3.

16. This line of questioning comes from Gray, *Love Unleashes Life*, 47–48.

writes, 'Time is reflected in our age. Why should our personhood be grounded in our age?'"[17]

"I still believe you are misrepresenting Baal," the god griped. "In his debate with Stephanie Gray, Singer said he would deny that an adult with a brain injury was a person with a right to life, too."[18]

"It's grating when you speak in the third person. Well, in that case, I would agree that he's not discriminating based on age. Instead, he's engaging in ableism, or discriminating against someone based on their lack of abilities. Of course, this actually goes against Singer's own goal of bringing more equality to the world. He even said in his essay on speciesism that 'it is an implication of this principle of equality that our concern for others ought not to depend on what they are like, or what abilities they possess.'"[19]

"Well, if you want to bring speciesism into it, perhaps you should consider Michael Tooley's article," Baal interrupted. "As he explains, to accept the idea that the right to life is based on being human as a moral principle would 'be akin to accepting as a basic moral principle the proposition that it is morally permissible to enslave black members of the species homo sapiens but not white members.'"[20]

"That seems like a bit of a jump," Chris frowned.

"Not at all," Baal shook his head. "We would agree that a difference in skin color is not morally relevant, right?"

"Sure," Chris nodded.

"Well, in the same way, Tooley is arguing that 'difference in species is not per se a morally relevant difference.'"[21]

"I'll have to think about that one for a bit," Chris conceded. "Can I get back to you with an answer tomorrow?"

"Sure. I'll make it really simple for you. I want you to tell me what you think makes the human fetus more valuable than the

17. Gray, *Love Unleashes Life*, 48.

18. Harvard Right to Life, "Peter Singer and Stephanie Gray Debate," 1:16:34–1:17:05.

19. Singer, "All Animals Are Equal," 431.

20. Tooley, "Abortion and Infanticide," 51.

21. Tooley, "Abortion and Infanticide," 51.

cows, pigs, and chickens you eat, which, as Singer argues, 'Come out well ahead of the fetus at any stage of pregnancy.'[22] We can assume he thinks those animals come out well ahead of the newborn as well."

"Noted," Chris nodded.

Suddenly, Sarah's phone chimed. She pulled it out and whistled. "Wow, I have been here two hours already. Derek's wondering where I am. I should get back up there." She paused and looked regretfully at Chris. "I'm still not sure I feel ready to make a decision."

"I am here tomorrow if you want to come by again," Chris offered.

"Yes. I want to hear your answer to the speciesism question," said Sarah.

"I will be here as well to make sure the conversation stays honest," Baal announced. "So long for now." He winked out of sight.

"I guess I am going to have to seriously rethink my atheism after meeting a god," Sarah mused.

"Oh, he's not a god. He just thinks he is," Chris replied.

"What do you mean?" Sarah raised an eyebrow.

"I'll explain later. Go see your husband and son."

Interlude

Sarah walked into the ICU and went up to the window that looked into the room where they were keeping Ian. Her breath caught in her throat. It was difficult to see her young son lying in a glass incubator with all the tubes going into him.

Strong arms encircled her and the familiar scent of Derek filled her nose. She leaned back against him, sighing.

"Where were you?" Derek asked.

"Down in the chapel, talking to the hospital chaplain," she replied.

"Finding religion?" Derek half-joked.

22. Singer, *Practical Ethics*, loc. 135.

"No, but I did have an interesting conversation with the chaplain about our situation."

"Great. And you probably got some pro-life propaganda about why it is wrong for us to let Ian die."

"He actually had some points I had never considered before about why Ian has the right to life."

"Ian's not a person. Nonpersons don't have a right to life."

"Did you know that most human rights documents actually say that all humans are persons with a right to life?"

Derek hesitated. "No, I didn't."

"And I know we always say a human has to be rational to be a person, but the chaplain showed how that could be a form of discrimination based on age or ability. And that type of discrimination is also a human rights violation."

"Wow, that chaplain sure did a number on your head," Derek sighed.

Sarah pried his arms off of her and spun around to glare at him. "You know, you're the second male today that suggested I can't think critically enough to avoid being brainwashed by another man."

That brought Derek up short. He realized he was being condescending. "I'm sorry, babe. I'm stressed out. We have to make a decision that is going to affect our lives in a major way no matter what we do."

"Which is why I would like to wait until after tomorrow before we decide whether to give Ian the surgery or not."

"What difference does a day make?"

"Someone else showed up. Someone on the pro-choice side. He asked a question I'd like to hear the chaplain's answer to."

"I dunno, babe . . . ," Derek groaned.

Sarah stuck out her jaw. "I'm sorry, did you think I was asking permission?"

Derek sagged. "I guess one more day can't hurt."

"Do you want to come and listen, too?"

"No. I don't think I would be able to stay as civil as you. You can give me the play-by-play later." Derek checked his watch. "It's almost 6:00 p.m. Let's go to the cafeteria and get some food."

"Sounds good to me," Sarah nodded.

Round 2

Sarah arrived bright and early the next morning with Tim Hortons coffee jugs, cups, and doughnuts.

Chris looked like he had been up all night. There were bags under his eyes and he was disheveled. But he seemed energized nonetheless.

"Oh, you are a life saver," he said as he took a cup and poured himself some coffee.

"I couldn't stand the thought of relying on vending machine coffee again." She eyed him up and down. "Did you sleep here or something?"

"No. When I know I have any sort of presentation or debate coming up, I'm usually up the whole night before preparing for it. As soon as Baal gets here, we can begin."

"I am here!" There was a thunder crash and Baal appeared by the ceiling again.

Chris and Sarah waved their hands and coughed. "You know, this is a no smoking area, right?" Chris asked.

"Very funny," Baal said. "Enough chitchat. I want you to prove to me that you have a good reason for denying animals a right to life!"

Chris flipped through some notes he had jotted down. "I have two points to make here. First, Tooley suggested that there is nothing morally relevant about the difference between species. But human society already recognizes there is a moral relevance."

"Oh, this I have to hear," said Baal.

"Christopher Kaczor gives several examples to back this up:

> First, there is a moral difference between a hit-and-run involving a squirrel and a hit-and-run accident involving a newborn human being, even if the baby killed were a

> mentally handicapped and orphaned newborn. Second, even though many people are vegetarians out of respect for the moral worth of animals, there is still an important difference between eating a hamburger and a Harold burger, even if Harold, due to his mental handicap, was no more intelligent than a cow . . . third . . . Although sexual mores have changed a great deal over the last few decades, it is wrong for human beings to have sexual intercourse with non-human animals.[23]

"These differences only make sense if there is something significant about humans, squirrels, and cows not being the same species."

"And what do you think that society is recognizing in humans?" Sarah asked.

"I think has to do with the personal nature that Francis Beckwith says is present 'from the moment a human being comes into existence regardless of whether it has the present exercisable capacity for, or is currently engaging in, personal acts.'[24]

"And this leads into my second point, which is that I am okay with eating the cows, chickens, and pigs that Singer mentions because it seems quite clear that they do not possess the same kind of rational nature that a human does.[25] I should say though that it doesn't mean I think it's impossible for any animal to have that nature. For example, a couple of years ago, I attended an exhibit at the Royal BC Museum on orca whales. It turns out that people are advocating for their personhood to be recognized. Orcas come very close to the level of rationality and self-awareness that humans have. This recognition would stop them from being hunted for meat or put in captivity. I support these measures."[26]

"Is there any hard evidence that humans have this rational nature?" asked Sarah.

23. Kaczor, *Ethics of Abortion*, loc. 24–25.

24. Beckwith, *Defending Life*, 161–62.

25. Singer, *Practical Ethics*, loc. 135.

26. Royal BC Museum, "Orcas: Our Shared Future."

"I think the fact that it's a normal part of being human to develop the kind of brains that make our level of rationality possible is good evidence of that nature," Chris replied.

Sarah's phone started ringing.

"Derek?" asked Chris.

She checked her caller ID. "No, my mom. The poor woman's been anxious for an update but I've just been too busy to call her. I should take this."

"Go ahead. We'll be here," Chris nodded.

Sarah smiled appreciatively, got up, and headed out of the chapel.

Interlude Part 2

Outside in the hospital parking lot, Sarah answered her phone. "Hey, mom!"

"Hi, sweetheart!" exclaimed her mom. "How are you holding up? Are you eating enough? Are you getting any sleep? How's Derek?"

"Woah, mom, one question at a time," said Sarah. "I'm hanging in there. I am eating regularly. I am averaging about five hours of sleep a night. And Derek has been my rock through this."

Her mom hesitated a moment, then asked what was really on her mind. "And Ian?"

"Still alive. I can't seem to make a decision about the surgery yet."

"I can't believe you would even consider letting him die."

"Really, mom? You raised me to be about as pro-choice as they come. Why are you squeamish now?"

Her mom sounded offended. "There is no need to kill him. I had you read Mary Anne Warren as a teenager. You know she points out that there are many other people out there who would be willing to adopt him even if he has Down's syndrome. If you let him die, you're not only depriving him of life, you're also depriving other people of the satisfaction of being able to adopt him."[27]

"There were people who would have been ready to adopt him when I was pregnant, too, mom. Abortion would have deprived them of that satisfaction as well. So where was your concern there?"[28]

"He isn't using your body anymore."

"Come on, mom. You have three kids of your own. Hell, you know babies don't stop using their parents' bodies after they're born."

"Well, the fact of the matter is, Sarah, that as Warren writes, 'Most of us value the lives of infants, and would greatly prefer to pay taxes to support foster care and state institutions for disabled children, rather than allow them to be killed or abandoned.'"[29]

"Well, then society is a bunch of hypocrites!" Sarah was shouting now. "Now, they are the ones imposing their morality on me and not trusting me as a woman to know what's best for me and my body. If you don't like infanticide, don't pay a doctor to kill your baby."

Her mom was silent for a moment. Finally, she said, "Obviously, you're upset. This isn't the best time for a debate. Just know I love you and I'm sending positive thoughts your way."

Sarah sighed and nodded. "Thanks, mom. I love you, too. I'll call you when we have more news." They hung up.

A Substantive Argument

"How did it go?" asked Chris when Sarah reentered the chapel.

"It went," Sarah said. "Typical mother-daughter drama in times of stress. I don't want to talk about it." She went and poured herself another cup of coffee, then picked up a Boston cream doughnut. "Where were we?"

27. Warren makes this point in "On the Moral and Legal Status of Abortion," 350.

28. Kaczor, *Ethics of Abortion*, loc. 45.

29. Warren, "On the Moral and Legal," 351.

"I was about to voice my opposition to Chris's rational nature view!" Baal announced.

"I'm ready!" Chris gave a thumbs up.

"Chris is basically arguing that what makes Ian more valuable than cows, pigs, or chickens is that his potential for rationality is greater. Therefore, he is a potential person. But as Singer argues, 'It does not follow that the fetus has a stronger claim to life. There is no rule that says that a potential X has the same value as an X or has all the rights of an X.'"[30]

"On the other hand," Baal continued, "If Chris really wants to say that it is morally relevant that Ian is a potential person, then I would ask him what he thinks should be done in the following scenario from Tooley. Imagine that at some point in the future, a chemical serum is invented that could cause a kitten's brain to grow and develop to the point where it is as rational as a human. Because of this serum, all kittens are potential persons. Chris, do you believe in that instance, that you would have a moral obligation to inject the kitten with that serum and initiate the process just because Mittens is now a potential person?"[31]

"No, I don't think I would."

"All right, now I would like to introduce what Tooley calls the 'symmetry principle.' He writes, 'If it is not wrong to refrain from initiating such a causal process, neither is it wrong to interfere with such a process.'"[32]

"I have to admit, that is a pretty good rebuttal," Chris blew out a breath.

Baal scratched his chest and then looked at his hand admiringly. "Thank you, I know."

"But it's a good rebuttal to a point pro-lifers aren't making," Chris added.

"Oh, this is absurd!" Baal snapped. "You're moving the goal post on Baal! You just went on and on about how, given enough time, human beings will develop into rational beings."

30. Singer, *Practical Ethics*, loc. 138.

31. Tooley, "Abortion and Infanticide," 61.

32. Tooley, "Abortion and Infanticide," 61.

"There's that third person again," Chris cringed. "Anyway, I am not arguing that it is Ian's potential for rationality. Nor am I saying he is a potential person. I'm saying he is valuable because of something he already has, his rational nature. And this makes him a person already, a person with potential."[33]

"Semantics," scoffed Baal.

"It's not semantics. It's the difference between someone possessing personhood already and not possessing it yet," Chris fired back. "As for the kitten analogy, Tooley's scenario is not as symmetrical as he is suggesting. As Kaczor argues, Tooley is failing to recognize the different types of potentiality a kitten and a newborn have. The kitten's potentiality is passive, dependent on the serum. The newborn's potential, on the other hand, is active, which "is nothing other than growth or maturation, a self-propelled, self-development. . . . If functioning rationally is the benchmark of respect, a being actively self-developing towards functional rationality . . . deserves a greater respect than a being with the passive potential to become a being actively self-developing towards functional rationality. . . . So, even if a rationality serum existed, it would not follow that killing a kitten would be the moral equivalent of killing . . . [a] newborn.'[34] Tooley has not really refuted the pro-life position at all."

"Is there hard evidence that the kitten's potential is only passive?" Sarah asked.

"Well, why isn't it rational like us?" asked Chris.

"Because it doesn't have a brain like us."

"Will it ever develop a brain like us without the serum?"

"No."

"The fact that it needs something outside itself to be different indicates to me that a kitten is a different kind of substance with its own way of developing," Chris concluded.[35] "Now, I have a question for you both. Why does it matter so much to you whether a newborn is conscious and rational?"

33. Kaczor uses this term in *The Ethics of Abortion*, loc. 7.

34. Kaczor, *Ethics of Abortion*, loc. 28.

35. This line of reasoning comes from Gray, *Love Unleashes Life*, 48–49.

Desiring a Better Future

"Well, for me, I care about consciousness because that means the baby can feel pain," Sarah explained.

"Okay, and what is the significance of that?"

"Well, I'm not a complete sadist!" Sarah exclaimed. "I don't want to cause Ian unnecessary suffering."

"Okay, and what about rationality?"

"That's easy," said Baal. "Because, as Valerie Tarico writes, I believe the right to life goes to 'beings who can feel pleasure and pain, preference and intention.'[36] And as Singer argues, 'Newborn babies cannot see themselves as beings that might or might not have a future, and so they cannot have a desire to continue living . . . if a right to life must be based on the capacity to want to go on living, or on the ability to see oneself as a continuing mental subject, a newborn baby cannot have a right to life.'[37]

"As far as I can tell, the only person who is having their desires thwarted is you, Sarah," Baal pointed out. "You desire to have a healthy baby that is not going to unduly burden you and your husband for the rest of your lives. It's your desires that we should be worrying about."

"Okay," Chris chimed in, "But do you think causing someone to suffer is the same as harming them, Sarah?"

"I feel like you think I should answer no."

"If you think about it, we all recognize that not all suffering involves being wronged and that you don't always suffer when you're wronged. Horn gives the following illustrations to help us see the point:

> A dentist who painfully drills a tooth hurts the patient, but does not *harm* him, because a dentist's act makes the patient better off by treating a medical problem. Likewise, some acts can harm a person without hurting them. If I steal an inheritance from someone who didn't know it existed, I haven't hurt him (he isn't sad about the lost

36. Tarico, "Why I Am Pro-Abortion," para. 12.

37. Singer, *Practical Ethics*, loc. 152.

> money), but I have harmed him. If a male nurse fondles an unconscious female patient, he hasn't hurt her, but he has harmed her, because she is worse off by having her body violated by a stranger.[38]

So, you may not hurt Ian by letting him die but you might still be wronging him.

"Also, basing the right to life on desires leads to some issues as well. I can think of people who we would normally believe have a right to life even though they no desire to live. For example, I know someone who was very depressed growing up. He wanted to die, not to live. Despite this, I still knew it was wrong to kill him. Also, some people are in comas because of an accident. We still believe they have a right to life even though they are not currently desiring to live. Finally, people's desires can become distorted. Think of the followers of Jim Jones. They desired to die because they believed that would ensure their salvation. But even though they desired to die, we still think it was a great tragedy that they all committed suicide under his leadership. I'm just saying I'm not sure that desires are sufficient for basing the right to life on."[39]

"The key difference," Baal interjected, "is that, as Tooley writes,

> An individual's right to X can be violated not only when he desires X, but also when he *would* now desire X were it not for one of the following: (i) he is in an emotionally unbalanced state; (ii) he is temporarily unconscious; (iii) he has been conditioned to desire the absence of X.

That is why your friend, the coma patient, and the follower of Jim Jones would still have a right not to be killed."[40]

"But don't you see what Tooley's doing?" Chris replied. "He's moved the goal post. As Beckwith explains, this assumes that the depressed person, coma patient, and cult member are the sorts of

38. Horn, *Persuasive Pro-Life*, 142.

39. This argument comes from suggested responses given by Tooley, "Abortion and Infanticide," 47–48.

40. Tooley, "Abortion and Infanticide," 48.

beings who ought to desire the right to life even when they currently don't. And if that's the case, Beckwith argues, then it's not their desires that ground their right to life but the sorts of beings they are, ones that would have had a proper desire under better circumstances. And of course, I could apply the same logic to Ian. He is the kind of being who would desire the right to life were it not for his stage of development or his disability."[41] Chris started laughing.

Baal grew annoyed. "What is so funny?"

"I just realized you and Michael Tooley handed us a new pro-life argument. The newborn baby is the kind of being who would desire the right to life were it not for his immaturity or handicap. Therefore, it is wrong to kill them. Thanks a lot, Baal and Tooley!"[42]

Sarah started laughing, too. "He's got you there, Baal."

Baal sniffed. "Don't gloat, Mr. Chaplain. It doesn't suit you."

After the laughter settled, Sarah asked, "Have you ever considered that you may be hurting and harming him by not letting him die?"

Chris raised an eyebrow. "What do you mean by that?"

"Well, what about his quality of life?" Sarah asked.[43]

"Have you ever heard of the group Not Dead Yet?" Chris asked.

Sarah shook her head. "No. Sounds like a bunch of Monty Python fans."

"They are a disability group that actively opposes euthanasia. They write that we should 'recognize that quality of life is not fixed—it varies depending on the presence or absence of help, pain management, love, respect and money.'[44] They believe, as Stepha-

41. Beckwith, *Defending Life*, 148.

42. This suggestion was made to me by Paul Chamberlain over coffee. Paul Chamberlain is a professor at Trinity Western Global and has a PhD in philosophy. We spent a good three hours discussing this argument.

43. Warnock and MacDonald mention that this is a concern in these cases in *Easeful Death*, 40.

44. Disability Link, "What Is Not Dead Yet," para. 8.

nie Gray Connors argues, that 'we should alleviate the suffering without eliminating the sufferer.'"[45]

"Yeah," replied Sarah, "but as Warnock goes onto to say, 'The severity of the effects of Down's Syndrome vary greatly, and it is impossible to tell at birth how severely affected a child will be.'"[46]

"Yes, that is true. But that uncertainty is why Connor goes onto say, 'We must never assume we know the future,' but we must also 'never assume it's always best when we take control.'[47] For example, let's imagine Ian had been born perfectly healthy. But then four years down the line, it strikes you that you don't know how much he will suffer in his life. He might develop cancer. He might have an accident that leaves him a quadriplegic. Worse yet, he might outlive you with no one to care for him.[48] Would it be justifiable to kill Ian at four years old for these reasons?"

"No, because he is a person with a right to life," replied Sarah.

"Okay, but do you see the problem there?" asked Chris. "By saying it's okay to kill Ian for the same reasons, people like Warnock are simply assuming that he is not a person with a right to life. This is called begging the question."[49]

It's a Christian Thing

Baal was starting to feel a little desperate. His superiors wanted the baby dead and they wanted Sarah to have a mark on her soul that would cause her future despair. He had one last card he could play. "Sarah, you're an atheist, right?"

"Well . . . maybe not so much anymore," Sarah said.

"Well okay, but you're still not a Christian, right?"

"That is true."

45. Connors, *Start With What*, loc. 18.

46. Warnock and MacDonald, *Easeful Death*, 44.

47. Connors, *Start with What*, loc. 92.

48. Warnock and MacDonald, *Easeful Death*, 44.

49. Rae, *Introducing Christian Ethics*, 65.

"Well, as Singer writes, 'It may be worth remembering that our present absolute protection of the lives of infants is a distinctively Christian attitude rather than a universal ethical value.'[50] Since you are not a Christian, you are not under any obligation to play by their rules."

"Right," Chris scoffed. "Maybe we should take morality lessons from the guy who slept with a cow on the night before he died instead."[51]

Sarah stared wide-eyed at Baal. "Did you really?"

Baal rolled his eyes. "He loves bringing that story up."

"You did it over a hundred times! And you got her pregnant! It wasn't like it was an accident!"[52]

"Guys, enough!" Sarah shouted.

"Sorry." Chris took a breath. "Before we get to the Christian prohibition of infanticide, let's remember what grounds it. As Klusendorf writes, parents 'have a duty to sustain our own offspring.'[53] C. S. Lewis has shown that this value was shared by Greeks, Hindus, Romans, Chinese, and Native Americans."[54]

"Oh yes, the Greeks and Romans," Baal snorted. "Such respecters of parental obligations. That's why, as Singer writes, 'Plato and Aristotle recommended the killing of deformed infants,' and 'Romans like Seneca, also thought infanticide the natural and humane solution to the problem posed by sick and deformed babies.'"[55]

"But, why should we think that points to a difference in moral values?" Chris pressed. "Why couldn't it simply point to a difference in circumstances?"[56]

"I think I can see where you're going with this," Sarah spoke up. "Parents knew the sick infant would have a hard, unforgiving

50. Singer, *Practical Ethics*, loc. 153.

51. Arnold and Beyer, *Readings from Ancient Near East*, 59.

52. Arnold and Beyer, *Readings from Ancient Near East*, 59.

53. Klusendorf, *Case for Life*, 188.

54. Lewis, *Abolition of Man*, 91–93.

55. Singer, *Practical Ethics*, loc. 154.

56. Chamberlain, *Can We Be Good*, 83.

life in those societies. And they knew that they themselves didn't have the resources to care for him. So, in their minds, ending the child's life was caring for him?"

"Precisely," Chris nodded. "Like Paul Chamberlain writes,

> It is possible that a group of people could have the same moral values or principles as we have and yet . . . because of vastly different circumstances in life, those values cause them to perform different actions from what we do—actions that would appear morally abhorrent to us until we understand why they do them.[57]

I would say that, in that case, we're not disagreeing about the fact that parents should care for their children. Rather, we are disagreeing about how they should care for their child."

"Okay, but I don't think that this situation really applies to me," said Sarah. "I know that there are resources out there that the Romans and Greeks didn't have that could make Ian's and my life easier. But I don't think I need to go to the effort yet because he is not a person with a right to life."

"You're right. In that case, I would say it's a difference in beliefs about reality, not circumstances," said Chris. "We both agree that a parent should care for a child that's a person. We just disagree over whether this particular child is a person."[58]

"You and Baal have both made such compelling arguments about whether Ian is a person or not," Sarah said. "What if I can't make up my mind about which side is right?"

"Then I would recommend that you let Ian live," said Chris.

"You mean pretend he's a person anyway?" Sarah asked.

"No, I mean, if you're not sure if the life of a valuable person is a stake, do what we normally do and err on the side of life. As Horn writes, 'After all, we wouldn't blow up a building if we thought there could still be people inside of it.'"[59]

57. Chamberlain, *Can We Be Good*, 83.

58. Chamberlain, *Can We Be Good*, 87.

59. Horn, *Persuasive Pro-Life*, 122.

The True Face of Baal

"Well, Sarah," Baal said, puffing out his chest, "it seems you have a choice. You can either rely on the authority of a god who showed up personally to tell you that it was okay to let Ian die. Or you can listen to a God who let a puny human show up to do his heavy lifting for him."

"You're definitely a supernatural being claiming to be a god. You might have even done some impressive signs and wonders. But you aren't a god," Chris replied.

"You said that yesterday," said Sarah. "Then what is he?"

"He's gone by many names. Paul Copan lists a few: 'goat demons' (Lev 17:7); 'strange gods . . . demons . . . gods' (Deut 32:16–21); 'demons . . . idols' (Ps 106:37–38).[60] Basically, he's a spawn of hell who's as interested in seeing innocent blood shed today as he was in biblical times."

"You can't prove I'm a demon," said Baal nervously.

"Actually, I can. Do you confess that Jesus is God come to earth in the flesh?"

"I don't do rhetorical questions."

"In the name of Christ, do you confess it?" Chris asked more forcefully.

Baal gritted his teeth. "I can't."

"Then as 1 John 3:5 says, 'And every spirit that does not confess Jesus is not from God; this is the Spirit of the Anti-Christ, of which you have heard is coming and now is already in the world.' In the name of Christ, I command you to leave this place."

Baal, now a hideous monster, vanished with a scream.

Sarah could only gape. "That thing wanted me to kill Ian?"

"And the person who is more powerful than that monster wants you to keep him. I can't force you to make a choice one way or the other, Sarah, but at least remember that more powerful person when you talk to the doctor today," Chris advised. They finished their coffee. Then Sarah thanked Chris, hugged him, and headed back to the ICU.

60. Copan, *Is God a Moral Monster?*, loc. 167.

Conclusion

Sarah sat down facing Derek and took his hands in hers. "Derek, I've reached a decision."

Derek nodded. "I'm ready."

"I want Ian to have the surgery."

"What?" Derek exploded.

"I can't be sure that Ian is not a person of moral worth. The most responsible thing to do is err on the side of life!"

Derek got up and began pacing. He brought up all the same objections to Ian being a person worthy of moral consideration that Baal had and she responded with Chris's points.

When he couldn't get anywhere with logic, Derek finally leaned against the wall and heaved a sigh. Not looking at her, he said, "Well you can keep him alive if you want to. But you'll be raising him on your own."

Sarah was stricken. She didn't want to lose Derek. But she also didn't believe she could raise a Down's syndrome baby on her own. "Really, you would leave us, just like that?"

"You have your choice. I have mine."

They sat in silence for half an hour until the doctor finally arrived. Sensing the tension, the doctor asked kindly, "Should I come back?"

"No," Sarah replied, shaking her head and standing up. "We've come to a decision?"

"And that is?"

Sarah felt the eyes of both Derek and the doctor on her. Looking at Ian one last time, hoping he could forgive her, she said "We decline the surgery."

Two days later, Ian died.

Essay 4

A Brainless Suggestion

According to Ruth Stirton, there was a shortage of organ donors in 2017. To rectify this problem, she suggests the possibility of engineering humans without brains so that we can harvest organs from them.[1] Her reasoning goes like this:

> The respect and moral value that human beings attract is due to their capacity for consciousness and feeling—the elements of personhood. We nurture consciousness and intelligence, and we protect the ability to develop consciousness once an entity with the capacity to develop consciousness comes into being. If we were able to genetically engineer brainless humans, then the reasons behind these protections no longer apply.[2]

As far as I can tell, Stirton's argument has three parts. First, she defines a person with moral value, who is worthy of respect, as someone who has the capacity for consciousness and feelings. Second, she draws out the implications. According to Stirton, a brainless human would have no consciousness or feelings. Therefore, according to Stirton, it wouldn't be worthy of respect. Third, she concludes that we could do things to brainless humans that

1. Stirton and Lawrence, "No Pain, All Gain," para. 8.
2. Stirton and Lawrence, "No Pain, All Gain," para. 6.

would not be permissible with humans who had the capacity for consciousness and feelings.

My thesis for this essay is simple: it would be immoral to engineer brainless humans so that we could harvest their organs. I will argue this by attempting to show that those humans are already valuable enough to be protected by Stirton's standards.

To begin with, I think that our western contemporary society would object to her suggestion. Philosopher Dan W. Brock does a great job articulating the reason why. He writes,

> One commentator has proposed human cloning for obtaining even lifesaving organs (Kahn 1989). After cell differentiation, some of the brain cells of the embryo or fetus would be removed so that it could then be grown as a brain-dead body for spare parts for its earlier twin . . . Most people would likely find this practice appalling and immoral, in part because here the cloned later twin's capacity for conscious life is destroyed *solely as a means* for the benefit of another.[3]

Of course, this is the same society that has bought into the pro-choice logic that the unborn are not persons because they are not conscious. Moreover, they seem to agree with David Benatar, who says that "those who exist (in the morally relevant sense) have interests in existing."[4] So, in my estimation, Western societal values are worse than useless in combating such a suggestion. They're the cause of it because people like Stirton are just applying their logic consistently. These clones would never have a chance to develop interests, and so they would not exist in a morally relevant sense. As Francis Beckwith explains, societal objections would only make sense if the engineered human is entitled to having higher brain functions independent of his desires.[5] Society would have to reject their criteria for what gives humans rights to properly oppose this practice. Yet, for many, their moral intuition that this practice should be opposed remains. So, what accounts for that intuition?

3. Brock, "Cloning Human Beings," E8.
4. Benatar, *Better Never to Have Been*, loc. 293.
5. Beckwith, *Defending Life*, 140.

I think the pro-life view of what makes humans valuable has the answer.

First, Stirton seems to be implying that early humans do not have the capacity for consciousness. What needs to be noted here is that there are two types of capacities: basic and immediate. Basic capacities, according to Robert P. George and Christopher Tollefsen, are the internal resources every human has to develop the "exercisable capacities for characteristically human functions."[6] Immediate capacities are the ability to exercise those functions.[7] It is true that early-stage humans do not have immediate capacities. But every human comes into existence with basic capacities, even if they are prevented from having later immediate capacities by some extrinsic cause. It is those basic capacities pro-lifers say that human value comes from and that we should base rights on.

Second, pro-lifers contend that it is simply not true that lacking consciousness, feelings, and desires makes you not a person. And for the most part, Western society agrees. To see this just requires a little reflection. As Marc Newman asks, "Do adults cease to be persons when they slip into unconsciousness?"[8] Most people would answer no. Of course, an adult is still a person, even if they are unconscious. But then, if a society can affirm that the adult human is a person even if they are unconscious, then it seems like special pleading to say that the embryo is not a person because they lack consciousness.

Third, it is not true that a human being's consciousness and feelings are what attracts our respect and moral values. Otherwise, to go back to the example of the unconscious adult, no one would bat an eye if we stole money from him or, even worse, killed him. But the fact is, we would still believe he was wronged if someone committed those crimes against him while he was unconscious. What this suggests is that in most cases, it is the bearer of consciousness that societies consider important, not consciousness itself.

6. George and Tollefsen, *Embryo*, loc. 1228.

7. George and Tollefsen, *Embryo*, loc. 1128.

8. Newman, *Contenders*, loc. 1725.

Stirton might reply that the unconscious adult has a brain. This means he has the capacity for consciousness and would feel fear over being killed or emotional pain over being robbed if he were not unconscious. But notice that at that point, it is not the adult's ability to be conscious or feel pain that commands our respect and moral values. In other words, it is not his immediate capacities to function in a certain way. It is what the unconscious adult is, namely, the type of being who would feel a certain way if not for his current circumstances. This would then further support the pro-life point that it is the bearer of consciousness that societies consider important, not consciousness itself. In the same way, embryos should command her respect and moral values.[9] For they are also the type of beings that would desire not to be enslaved for their organs if they had time to develop or hadn't been engineered to be brainless.[10] (Likely, they would also desire not to be robbed of their brains as well.)

Fourth, the embryo is already valuable. As Newman goes onto explain, "The nature of the human to be a rational being should confer that protection. Even in such instances where human expressions of rationality are inhibited . . . the nature of the being is still ordered to be rational."[11] By "ordered," he means that humans are programmed so that they naturally develop brains that allow them to be rational. In fact, Stirton as much admits that these humans have this nature when she talks about having to engineer them so that they don't grow brains.

Finally, what makes engineering them to be brainless wrong is that we are intentionally disabling human beings. Christopher Kaczor writes, "As Aristotle noted, rationality plays a constitutive role in human flourishing, so a lack of ability to function rationally

9. By brainless human beings here, I mean those who have been specifically engineered by human intervention. If the human became brainless through a disability, this criticism would not apply.

10. This is largely based on Beckwith's response to David Boonin's desires account of moral rights in *Defending Life*, 148.

11. Newman, *Contenders*, loc. 1744.

constitutes a grave disability for a mature human being."[12] Therefore, I offer a defeater for Stirton's position with the following syllogism.

1. Even embryos who have not not developed brains are valuable.
2. Valuable humans deserve human rights.
3. Therefore, embryos who have not yet developed brains deserve human rights.

For these reasons, we should not engineer embryos to be brainless so that we can harvest their organs. But even if someone did, those brainless humans should still be treated with respect.

12. Kaczor, *Disputes in Bioethics*, loc. 7.

Essay 5

An Out-of-This-World Problem

THE YEAR IS 2037. The UN has just received an unexpected, yet very exciting, visitor. His name is Anton. Such a normal sounding name belies the most amazing fact about him: Anton is not from this world.

Anton is from the planet Antonia. He crash-landed on Earth fifty years ago with his crew of fifty. They are called the Antonyms. They are clearly not human. They resemble gigantic red ants. But they can communicate in English and they walk around on their hind feet.

They had not planned on revealing themselves. They hoped to either be rescued by others of their kind or remain in hiding until they died off. However, their members have begun suffering from a horrible disease that they had brought from their home world. It causes their bodies to melt down into a pile of goo. It is a slow and painful process that could last for a year.

If they could get back home to Anton, there would be a cure, but Earth technology is not up to the challenge of curing them. What Anton is requesting is to be given access to Medical Assistance in Dying so that his people do not have to die in excruciating agony any longer. The UN now has to decide whether to give MAID to them or not. This essay will first explore the ethical challenges that the UN would face making such a decision. Second, it will explore the different courses of actions they could take. Third it will outline a couple of ethical theories that the UN could look to for guidance. Fourth, it will consider some biblical principles that would be relevant in this scenario. Fifth, it will discuss which ethical theory I think is best. Finally, I will suggest the course of action I think the UN should take in accordance with that principle.

The Ethical Challenges Involved

There are at least three potential ethical challenges that could arise. The first is the question of who gets the kinds of rights the aliens are asking for. But in answering this question, things get complicated at the get-go. Princeton philosopher Peter Singer writes that the discovery of such aliens in our midst would lead to some other prior questions: "What moral status would extraterrestrials have? Would we have obligations to them? Would they have rights? And would our answers depend on how intelligent they are?"[1] MAID has generally been construed as a human right, which would seem to disqualify the Antonyms from receiving it. On the other hand, they seem equal to us in level of intelligence, self-awareness, and communication ability. So, pointing to those qualities might be a good argument for extending the same moral consideration to them.[2]

Singer goes onto point out that if we grant these rights to the aliens on the basis of those abilities, it will have implications for how we treat our fellow humans as well.

> For then we have to consider human beings who fail the test—as both human infants, and humans with profound intellectual disability, do. Surely they have interests that need to be considered, whether or not they possess, or have the potential to develop, higher cognitive capacities.[3]

1. Singer, *Ethics in the Real World*, 404.
2. Singer, *Ethics in the Real World*, 406.
3. Singer, *Ethics in the Real World*, 406.

What Singer is getting at is that if intelligence, self-awareness, and the ability to communicate are the determining factors in whether a group has rights, then that might solve the problem of whether to give the Antonyms the same rights. However, it would also create new problems by excluding human beings, such as unborn and newborn babies and the mentally handicapped, who can't think or speak. That would be morally troubling to some people.

The second ethical challenge that could arise from giving the Antonyms MAID is the concern of keeping humans safe. Anton and his people would have been on Earth long enough to understand human culture. If they were to receive MAID, they would know that it was not intended as a direct assault on them but rather an act of mercy. However, let's imagine that a rescue team from their home world finally arrived to bring them back. To complicate things, let's imagine that the rescue team does not know any of the human languages, so there is no way to communicate with them about what Earth's intentions were in administering MAID. They also do not have the practice of MAID on their planet because they have the technology to cure most diseases. This means they have no frame of reference. All of this makes our act of mercy killing look like homicide to them. This could be construed as an act of war by Earth and lead to the aliens raining down retribution on the planet. We might end up obliterated at worst or enslaved at best.

Third, it involves the ethical challenge of the practice of MAID itself. For some, allowing this practice is clearly the right thing to do. Philosopher Jeff McMahan explains the justification this way:

> Consider a case in which a person's life is not worth living: it is and will remain dominated by pain and suffering that cannot be alleviated and are not counterbalanced by compensating goods . . . if it is true that pain and suffering are in themselves bad, it seems that a life

> that contains little or nothing but pain and suffering . . . cannot be worth enduring.[4]

This reasoning is easy to apply to the Antonyms' case. They are all going to be melted alive. Even worse, because their biology is so different from ours, giving them sufficient pain medication is difficult. They can't go out, they can't eat, and they can't even sleep. In short, they don't seem to have a lot to live for. So why not give them a way out?

For others, though, suicide is never the right option. Blaise Alleyne and Jonathon Van Maren point out that we normally have an instinct to prevent suicide. Yet, when someone is terminally ill, countries like Canada, the US, and the Netherlands suddenly claim that we have a fundamental responsibility to assist the person in killing themselves. This, they say, raises a question for the pro-euthanasia side: Who gets suicide assistance and who gets suicide prevention? What makes it harm in one case and help in another? For them, it wouldn't matter if the Antonyms are physically healthy or dying. Our duty to them is to provide suicide prevention.[5]

Optional Courses of Action

There are four courses of action that the UN could take to help the Antonyms. First, they could find a basis for rights that included the aliens *and* humans regardless of their age or abilities. Along with Marc Newman, I would argue that "the nature of the human to be a rational being should confer . . . protection," such as rights.[6] Since the Antonyms are intelligent, self-aware, and able to communicate, it would seem that they have a rational nature as well. That could then be the basis for extending to them the same protections. This rationale would avoid unjust discrimination.

4. McMahan, *Ethics of Killing*, loc. 458.

5. Alleyne and Van Maren, *Guide to Discussing Assisted Suicide*, loc. 126, 122, 1265.

6. Newman, *Contenders*, loc. 1744.

Second, the UN could simply give them the MAID procedure that they are asking for. A common method is "for physicians to assist their patients . . . by prescribing a lethal dose of some medicine."[7] This would respect the Antonyms' choice to die. Moreover, it would put an end to their pointless suffering.

Third, the UN could deny their request for MAID but still try and assist them by putting them in palliative care. The World Health Organization defines palliative care as

> an approach that improves the quality of life of patients (adults and children) and their families who are facing problems associated with life-threatening illness. It prevents and relieves suffering through the early identification, correct assessment and treatment of pain and other problems, whether physical, psychosocial or spiritual.[8]

Palliative care may not be able to treat the Antonyms' pain right away. However, the alien visitors can be given support by the people around them and they can be shown that they still have a purpose in life. And for those times where the pain is absolutely unbearable, there is the option of palliative sedation.[9] As Van Maren explains, it "may have the foreseen but unintended side effect of shortening the life."[10] According to the doctrine of double effect, however, the intent in palliative sedation, unlike in suicide, is not to kill the patient. It is to manage their pain.[11] The rationale for this action would be to remain consistent on society's stance on suicide being bad. Moreover, not putting the Antonyms to death would avoid the risk of misunderstanding if other Antonyms showed up. Deciding on a course of action can be tricky. Thankfully, there are different ethical theories that could help find the right one.

7. McMahan, *Ethics of Killing*, loc. 458.

8. World Health Organization, "Palliative Care," para. 9.

9. Alleyne and Van Maren, *Guide to Discussing Assisted Suicide*, loc. 555, 1115.

10. Alleyne and Van Maren, *Guide to Discussing Assisted Suicide*, loc. 1115.

11. Alleyne and Van Maren, *Guide to Discussing Assisted Suicide*, loc. 1115.

A Social Contract Answer

Jonathan Wolff explains the social contract theory of ethics this way: "This concept of morality presents moral behavior as a type of agreement by which each of us indirectly pursues our self-interest. It also has the great advantage that it seems to base morality on human agreement."[12] To resolve the question of whether to give the Antonyms MAID, the UN could vote. If the majority said yes, they'd give MAID to the Antonyms. If the majority said no, the UN wouldn't.

A Utilitarian Answer

Utilitarianism, according to Craig E. Johnson,

> is based on the premise that ethical choices should be based on their consequences . . . the best decisions generate the most benefits, as compared with their disadvantages, and benefit the largest number of people.[13]

For those in the pro-MAID camp, they might point to benefits such as ending the needless suffering of the Antonyms, and the freeing up of already scarce medical resources that could be used to care for people who want it.[14] For those who oppose MAID, they might point out that we can't be sure that the aliens will be better off if we kill them. After all, if doctors do their job properly, they can't come back and report on it. Second, there's the potential threat of war. Third, it could lead to Antonyms taking MAID even if they don't want to. For their leaders might force them to, thinking that it's better than using up Earth's limited resources on a hopeless case.[15]

12. Wolff, *Introduction to Moral Philosophy*, 109.

13. Johnson, *Meeting the Ethical Challenges*, 144–45.

14. Singer, *Ethics and the Real World*, 126.

15. Pearcey, *Love Thy Body*, 90. Pearcey mentions that many people request physician assisted suicide because they fear needing help and being a burden on the people around them.

Christian Themes and Biblical Principles to Help

The discovery of an alien race that is sentient like us would probably be alarming to Christians at first due to things we've been told. After all, as C. S. Lewis writes,

> If the universe is teeming with life, this . . . reduces to absurdity the Christian claim—or what is thought to be the Christian claim—that man is unique, and the Christian doctrine that to this one planet God came down and was incarnate for us men and our salvation.[16]

According to the reasoning of some, to be unique, humans would have to be the only species of their kind, completely unlike anything else. Compared to most other life forms in creation, we are unique by virtue of our intelligence. Finding another life form equal in intelligence to us would seem to threaten that standing. Moreover, if they are sinful like us, then it would seem that God would have to incarnate as an Antonym and die for their sins as well.

But Lewis assures us that we do not need to be troubled for a couple of reasons.

1. Christianity does not necessarily demand an anthropocentric view of the universe. While God loves man, and incarnated and died to save man, that does not prove that man is the sole end of nature.[17]
2. The incarnation would only be in conflict with the aliens' existence if we knew that the Antonyms were fallen and in need of redemption. But for all we know, they might not need redemption, or they may have already been redeemed. We couldn't know that for sure either.[18]

Despite these questions, I think that the Bible does tell us a few things clearly.

16. Lewis, "Dogma and the Universe," 26–27.
17. Lewis, "Dogma and the Universe," 30.
18. Lewis, "Dogma and the Universe," 30.

1. All suffering and sickness in creation are a part of the fall. Since the Antonyms are part of creation, they are experiencing those effects (Rom 8:22–29).
2. As John Jefferson Davis writes, "While the Bible never explicitly condemns suicide, every instance of suicide in the Bible is directly associated with the person's spiritual collapse, from Saul to Judas."[19] If the Antonyms are requesting suicide, they are obviously experiencing spiritual despair over their condition.
3. The Bible is clear that we are not to murder (Exod 20:13; Deut 5:17).[20]
4. As Scott B. Rae writes, "The Bible is clear that the community has an obligation to protect the most vulnerable among us."[21] It is hard to imagine anyone more vulnerable than the Antonyms who are on Earth. They are visitors from a strange world, at our mercy, and in need of help. For these reasons, those following the Bible could not justify meeting the Antonyms' request for MAID.

Which Ethical Theory Would I Choose?

I would not rely on either social contract theory or Utilitarianism. Social contract theory amounts to might equals right, for as long as more people agree with an action than disagree, it is "moral." But on this model, we could justify rape, theft, and murder as long as enough people thought it should be allowed.

As for Utilitarianism, it has two major problems. First, without being able to see the future, we can't actually know what the final consequences of an action will be. You might save someone's life, which makes them happy for a short time. But if they go and murder a hundred people, then the consequences of your actions

19. Davis, *Evangelical Ethics*, 198.
20. Rae, *Introducing Christian Ethics*, 114.
21. Rae, *Introducing Christian Ethics*, 114.

were actually bad because you made more people unhappy, and your good work becomes evil. Second, whether consequences look good or bad has a subjective element. If you're a criminal, going to prison looks bad because you lose your freedom as a consequence. If you're a victim, the criminal going to jail looks positive because you are getting justice.

I prefer a third option, which I think lines up with the idea that the Bible gives us moral principles to follow: deontology. Johnson explains that this theory holds that "people should do what is morally right no matter the consequences. Deontological ethicists argue that we ought to make choices based on our duty."[22] Still the question remains of what our duty is to the Antonyms in this situation.

The Course of Action I Would Take

The action that I believe the UN should take is putting the sick and dying Antonyms in palliative care. There are several reasons for this. First, it treats their request for suicide for what it really is: a cry for help.[23] Van Maren writes that "experts have stated throughout the literature on suicide prevention that suicidal despair is *always a symptom of some other unmet need.*"[24] If the Antonyms are requesting suicide, it might be because their pain is not being adequately managed. If we could figure out a way to eliminate their pain through pain killers or sedation, they may no longer want MAID. Second, this would avoid violating our duty not to murder innocent people. Third, it would fulfill our duty to care for the weak and innocent. Fourth, it could provide a chance to share the gospel with them if they had not heard it and assure them that God loves them and has a plan for them, even if it is hard to fathom it, given their sickness.

22. Johnson, *Meeting the Ethical Challenges*, 147–48.

23. Alleyne and Van Maren, *Guide to Discussing Assisted Suicide*, loc. 660.

24. Alleyne and Van Maren, *Guide to Discussing Assisted Suicide*, loc. 653.

Conclusion

For the reasons given, I do not think the UN should give the Antonyms access to MAID. Instead, the UN should ensure the Antonyms are looked after through palliative care.

Essay 6

A Strong Attempt at Defending Abortion

A review of David Boonin's *A Defense of Abortion* and *Beyond Roe*

CHRIS SLAMMED HIS LAPTOP shut and sighed heavily.

His wife, Amy, not completely unused to these exasperated outbursts, poked her head around the corner of the kitchen. "What's wrong now, babe?"

"I spent five days writing up a response to some pro-choice hack after he Gish galloped me with a hundred points in favor of abortion," Chris ranted. "He gets back to me in all of five minutes and basically just says, 'Well, you must hate women.'"

"That sucks. I'm sorry you're frustrated," said Amy, once again feeling vindicated in not letting herself get sucked into these online free-for-alls.

"I just give up," Chris exclaimed, as he sagged back in his chair. "Pro-choicers do not seem to be interested in understanding our arguments or having a real conversation."

There was a clap of thunder and smoke filled the apartment. A tall man with curly brown hair appeared in the air. He wore a horned helmet and carried a mace in one hand and a lightning bolt in the other.

"Not so fast, Apologetics Man! Behold, it is I . . . ," he began to intone.

"Yes, yes, I know who you are. Come to kick me while I'm down, Baal?" Chris asked.

Baal was miffed at being interrupted. "Hardly. I am here to do you a favor. I am going to introduce you to the work of a pro-choice philosopher who is everything you could hope for. His name is David Boonin."

Boonin's Thesis and Methodology

"I think I've come across that name in the pro-life books I've read," said Chris. "Who is he?"

"He is an associate professor of philosophy at the University of Colorado at Boulder," Baal explained. "He has written two books on the subject of abortion: *A Defense of Abortion* and *Beyond Roe*, along with other books, such as *The Non-Identity Problem and the Ethics of Future Persons* and *Dead Wrong*."

Amy, remarkably unfazed by a pagan god appearing in her living room, leaned against the wall and asked, "What makes him different than anyone else Chris has talked to?"

"A couple of things," Baal replied. "First, he actually admits that the unborn are humans. In the introduction to *A Defense of Abortion*, he talks about how his office is full of pictures of his son Eli at different stages of Eli's life. In the top drawer of Boonin's desk is a particularly special picture. It is a sonogram of Eli twenty-four weeks before he was born.[1] Boonin writes, "There is no doubt in my mind that this picture, too, shows the same little boy at a very early stage in his physical development. And there is no question that the position I defend in this book entails that it would have been morally permissible to end his life at this point."[2]

Amy made a face like she'd bit into something sour. "Well, that's a pretty chilling admission."

1. Boonin, *Defense of Abortion*, xiii–xiv.
2. Boonin, *Defense of Abortion*, xiv.

"Yeah, but on the other hand, it's kind of refreshing to hear a pro-choicer be so brutally honest about what he's advocating for," Chris shrugged. "So, what are his main arguments?"

Baal floated down and sat on the rocking chair. "Boonin understands that for everyone to get on board with abortion, he would have to show that it is morally justifiable for it to be legal. He defines an action as morally permissible if no one has a valid claim against him committing it. His thesis is that the fetus has no valid claim against the woman aborting him or her. The fetus may be the same human through every stage of development, but that is not enough to endow him or her with the right to life. His method is called 'reflective equilibrium.'"[3]

At Amy's questioning look, Chris explained, "Reflective equilibrium was a method put forward by John Rawls. Basically, you start with certain judgments, such as religious toleration is good or racism is bad.[4] Then, according to Rawls, 'We collect such settled convictions . . . and try to organize the basic ideas and principles implicit in those convictions into a coherent political conception of justice.'"[5]

Amy snapped her fingers. "So, for example, if we believe that religious toleration is good, we would forbid hate crimes like fire-bombing a mosque?"

"Precisely," Chris nodded. "And more to the point of abortion, if we believe that murdering innocent human beings is wrong, we would make abortion illegal."

Is the Fetus a Moral Subject?

"We're getting ahead of ourselves," Baal interjected. "Before you make such a claim, you should at least hear why Boonin does not think abortion is tantamount to murder. Chapter 2 and the first half of chapter 3 show why pro-life arguments for the right to life

3. Boonin, *Defense of Abortion*, 4–5.
4. Rawls, *Political Liberalism*, 8.
5. Rawls, *Political Liberalism*, 8.

of the unborn do not work. Then, in the second half of chapter 3, he argues for when he thinks the unborn become worthy of moral consideration."

Boonin's Conception of the Conception Criteria

Chris nodded. "Right. Walk me through his objections."

"Boonin summarizes and critiques nine different arguments for why the fetus has the right to life from conception onwards: 1) the parsimony argument, 2) the species essence argument, 3) the kindred species argument, 4) the sanctity of human life argument, 5) the slippery slope argument, 6), the potentiality argument, 7) the essential property argument, 8) the future like ours argument, and 9) the probability argument. Any of those sound interesting to you?" Baal inquired.

"How about we start with the slippery slope?" Chris suggested.

"Sure," Baal replied. "Let me begin by asking you a question. What is the main reason that you reject the pro-choice side's proposed thresholds for when personhood begins?"

Chris mulled that over. "I guess it's because, as philosopher Nancy Pearcey writes, the characteristics they choose as the marks of personhood

> emerge gradually. They are not traits that someone either does or does not have. They are matters of degree—*quantitative* differences. What we do not find is a clear *qualitative* transition point for the momentous transformation from a non-person to a person.[6]

In other words, there's not a big neon sign that appears and says 'This is now a person.' This opens up the possibility that the unborn is already a person with rights before the abortion takes place. So, their criteria are too tenuous to risk something as valuable as human life on."

"So, where do you place the personhood threshold at?" Baal wanted to know.

6. Pearcey, *Love Thy Body*, 53.

"Conception," Chris and Amy answered in unison.

"Well, then, I think you are judging the pro-choice side by an unfair double standard," Baal declared.

"What do you mean by that?" Amy asked.[7]

"I mean that given your reasons for rejecting pro-choice thresholds, you must be choosing conception because, as Boonin writes, you think it is 'the only place where there is a fundamental discontinuity in your developmental history.'"[8] Baal wagged a finger. "But that is not accurate."

"How did you come to that conclusion?" Amy pressed.[9]

"By looking at the science, of course," Baal sniffed. "As Boonin shows, conception is not some momentary event but one that takes place over twenty-two hours and has multiple stages."[10]

"How did he come to the conclusion that that is what we are arguing though?" Amy asked. "Does he cite any apologetics material?"

Baal became a bit unsure. "Well, no. He is using reflective equilibrium to deduce that is what you're arguing."

"Well, unfortunately, the reflective equilibrium method has led him astray here," Chris said. "Perhaps pro-lifers have used misleading terminology in the past and spoken of the 'moment of conception.' If so, that's our bad. But even pro-life apologist Francis Beckwith talks about how there are different stages in the conception process. He further acknowledges that there is a disagreement about the precise moment when conception is complete and a human embryo is present."[11]

"So, why do you guys choose conception as the point where personhood begins?" Baal demanded.

"Because that is when what Hendrik van der Breggen describes as a 'genetically distinct, self-governing, whole living

7. Koukl suggests starting with this question in *Tactics*, loc. 65.

8. Boonin, *Defense of Abortion*, 36.

9. Koukl, *Tactics*, loc. 84.

10. Boonin, *Defense of Abortion*, 37.

11. Beckwith, "Defending Abortion Philosophically," 229.

organism/entity that belongs to the human species' is present.[12] So, to rebut what we're saying, Boonin doesn't need to show that conception is a continuous event. He needs to show that the unborn human is not a person."

"Hm . . . ," Baal seemed thrown off for a second and had to reconsider his plan of attack. Finally, he snapped his fingers. "Of course. How silly of me. I should have started with the parsimony argument. You guys are basing personhood on being a member of the human species."[13]

"Well, that's not quite it either . . . ," Chris began.

"And Boonin even grants that it is quite parsimonious! If you were to gather ten people that we all agreed had a right to life in a room, the one thing that they would likely all have in common is that they were human![14] Moreover,

> the property of being a member of the human species can plausibly be characterized as morally relevant, since the human species itself can plausibly be characterized as superior to other species in terms of a number of important properties, such as rationality, linguistic ability, and so on, that in turn can plausibly be characterized as morally relevant.[15]

"Okay, but if you would allow me to explain . . . ," Chris tried again.

"Don't interrupt, it's rude," Baal snapped.

Chris held up his hands. "Sorry."

"The problem is that suggestion leads to implications that pro-lifers would find absurd. Imagine that a DNA test was done on the ten people in that room and it turned out that one of the men was an alien from another planet. He has all the same properties that we think make humans superior to other species. The only thing that sets him apart is that he has different DNA. It is hard to

12. van der Breggen, *Untangling Popular Pro-Choice Arguments*, loc. 7.

13. Boonin, *Defense of Abortion*, 22.

14. Boonin, *Defense of Abortion*, 22.

15. Boonin, *Defense of Abortion*, 22.

imagine that you would say he does not have a right to life and that it is okay for us to kill him."[16]

"You're right. I wouldn't," Chris nodded.

"Then, that shows that personhood and the right to life cannot be based on human species membership!" Baal declared.[17]

"This is a red herring!" Chris blurted out.[18]

Baal came up short. "What do you mean?"

"I mean that pro-lifers are not basing personhood and right to life on being human!" Chris explained. "Boonin is jumping on everything that we're saying as if it is a separate argument for personhood when it's really all part of the scaffolding that Beckwith says is necessary to appreciate and understand our argument."[19]

"You could have said something earlier." Baal groused.

"I tried!" Chris exploded, red in the face.

"Boys, calm down," Amy said, knowing her husband could have a temper. "Chris, why don't you explain what you mean, then."

Chris took a deep breath praying to the real God to give him the strength. "Look, there are three stages to the pro-life argument. The first is to establish what the unborn are biologically. The second stage is to establish that they are immediately persons from conception onward."

"How would you define a person, then?" asked Baal.

"Like Patrick Lee, I would say that 'a person can be defined as an "individual with a rational nature." Every individual with a rational nature is an entity whom we ought to respect, and whose good or fulfillment we ought to will for his or her own sake rather than treat as a mere means.'"[20]

"What do you mean by nature exactly?" Baal asked.

"Think of it as our internal programming," Chris explained. "As Lee and Robert P. George explain, 'From conception onward, the human embryo is fully programmed, and has the active

16. Boonin, *Defense of Abortion*, 22–23.

17. Boonin, *Defense of Abortion*, 23.

18. Beckwith, *Defending Life*, 161.

19. Beckwith, "Defending Abortion Philosophically," 231.

20. Lee, *Abortion and Unborn Human Life*, loc. 5.

disposition, to develop himself or herself to the next mature stage of a human being.'[21] So, we know they are programmed by a rational nature because humans naturally grow the type of brain that allows them to behave in a rational way.

"We further believe that we are persons from the moment of conception because we argue that human persons are essentially human organisms. As Lee explains, that means that a person cannot come into being or cease to exist apart from when the organism begins to exist or ceases to be. Take my dog, Buffy, for example." The Siberian Husky that was lying on the couch perked up at the mention of her name. When no treats were forthcoming, she went back to sleep. "A dog is what Buffy is while the color of her fur and her ability to run are properties that she has. Her gray color—that is, the gray color of her fur—may have been around before she was born, and it may exist long after the day she sadly dies. But since a dog is what she is, Buffy came to be when the dog that she is came to be. Likewise, since a human organism is not a property that I have but what I am, the time that I came to exist was at the time the organism began to exist. And I will only cease to exist when the organism ceases to. Since all human organisms begin to exist at conception, the human person begins at conception."[22]

"So, that is your reason for why it would be okay to kill the alien?" Baal inquired. "He's not human so he does not have a rational nature?"

"No, he very well could. There's nothing in this argument that requires that only humans have a rational nature. And like Beckwith argues, if another race with a rational nature was found on Earth or another planet, like a Vulcan or a Klingon, pro-lifers would fight for their right to life from the time they are conceived as well."[23]

"Well, you and Boonin may have to agree to disagree there. Why don't we move onto his argument for when human rights begin?" Baal suggested.

21. George and Lee, "Acorns and Embryos," para. 17.

22. Lee, *Abortion and Unborn Human Life*, 6.

23. Beckwith, *Defending Life*, 162.

"I'm game," Chris shrugged.

If I Only Had a Brain

"As I explained, the first half of chapter 3 deals with other post conception criteria that people have put forward," Baal told them. "This includes when the fetus implants in the uterus, when they begin to look human, when they begin to move, when their movement is detected, and initial brain activity. He disagrees with those criteria as well."

"We do, too," Amy chimed in. "Making those the criteria for personhood would be basing personhood on a fetus's level of development, and that's what pro-lifers are trying to avoid."

"Okay, then let's move on to when Boonin himself thinks that humans attain the right to life: when organized cortical brain activity is present."

"What's organized cortical brain activity?" Amy asked.

"According to Boonin, 'organized cortical brain activity refers to the electrical activity in the cerebral cortex of the sort that produces recognizable EEG readings . . . ample evidence . . . suggest[s] that it does begin to occur sometime between the 25th and 32nd week.'"[24]

"So, since the majority of abortions happen before the twenty-week mark of pregnancy, the vast majority of them would not violate the rights of a human with a right to life," Chris figured.[25]

"Not bad for a pro-lifer," Baal smirked.

"And why is cortical brain activity being present so important?" Chris asked, ignoring the barb.

"Because Boonin believes that people are only worthy of moral consideration once they have desires about how their lives should go. And they can only have such desires when they are conscious. Humans are not conscious until they have organized

24. Boonin, *Defense of Abortion*, 115.

25. Boonin, *Defense of Abortion*, 115.

cortical brain activity.[26] He adds, 'One implication of this account of the wrongness of killing, then, is that the fetus does not acquire the moral standing that you and I have prior to the point at which it has such activity.'"[27]

Amy had always suspected philosophers were a bit out of touch with reality, and this just confirmed it for her. "It's not just the fetuses who aren't going to have moral standing on this view!" she exploded. "A newborn baby isn't going to have awareness of his desires. Neither is someone who is in a coma. So, are we allowed to kill them?"[28]

"Boonin knew that people were going to say that. He has a ready response." Baal clasped his hands behind his back and looked off into space as if giving a lecture. "He makes a distinction between two kinds of desires: occurrent and dispositional. Neither the newborn baby or the comatose patient have occurrent desires or ones that they are consciously entertaining. But they do have dispositional desires, or desires that they just don't happen to be thinking about at the moment. Those desires would likely include not wanting to be killed. It is those dispositional desires that can ground the rights of a newborn or a comatose patient."[29]

"There's another side to this, though," Amy pointed out. "What about the person who is depressed and wants to end his life. Would we then be justified in killing him?"[30]

"Another good question," Baal conceded. "Once again, the answer is no. For there are two more kinds of desires that Boonin distinguishes between: actual and ideal desires. Actual desires are the ones you are currently having. Ideal desires are the desires you would have in better circumstances. If the depressed person were not actually depressed, he would desire to live. It is that ideal desire that we should respect."[31]

26. Boonin, *Defense of Abortion*, 125–26.
27. Boonin, *Defense of Abortion*, 126.
28. Beckwith, "Defending Abortion Philosophically," 237.
29. Boonin, *Defense of Abortion*, 122–23.
30. Beckwith, "Defending Abortion Philosophically," 238.
31. Boonin, *Defense of Abortion*, 124.

The Problem of Posthumous Rights

"Well, Boonin has certainly tried to cover all the angles, but I think he is contradicting himself," Chris mused.

"Contradicting himself how?" Baal sneered. "He's not saying that only people with desires have rights while saying people without desires have rights at the same time!"

"Well, isn't he, though?" Chris asked. "Amy and I were talking about wills the other day. She told me that when she dies, she wants her organs to be harvested so that they can go to someone in need of a transplant. Imagine that on the day she dies, though, I just have her cremated, organs and all. Now Boonin says in another book that 'it is possible for an act to make things go worse for a person in a way that generates a moral reason against doing it even if the act takes place after the person is dead.'[32] But Amy would not have cortical brain activity and therefore would not be conscious if she was dead. That means that she would have no desires. So, wouldn't she lose her moral standing?"

"Not necessarily," Baal shrugged. "You're talking about his 'case for unfelt harm.' He would argue that you are harming Amy by cremating her and not giving away her organs because she had a desire that her organs go to someone else who needs them. While she may not be aware of it, her desires are still being frustrated.[33] Perhaps they are not her actual desires, but they are ideal desires that she would have if she wasn't dead."

"Well, I agree with him that you can be harmed even if you do not consciously experience that harm," Chris interjected. "And therein lies the contradiction. In *A Defense of Abortion*, you need to have the capacity for desires. In *Dead Wrong*, you don't need that capacity at all. His judgment seems to assume that Amy is a being of a certain sort that would desire to have her posthumous desires respected, even when she does not actively desire them.[34] And as Beckwith argues, 'Then, it is not *desire* that grounds the

32. Boonin, *Dead* Wrong, 2.

33. Boonin, *Dead Wrong*, 11.

34. Beckwith, *Defending Life*, 148.

right to life, but the nature of the sort of being that would have this correct desire . . . or will have this correct desire when it reaches a certain level of maturity and is functioning properly.'"[35]

The Problem of the Buddhist Monk

"Oh, there's another issue that could arise," Amy exclaimed.

"What have you got, Amy?" Chris asked.

"When I was in Bible college, I learned about Buddhism," said Amy. "Central to Buddha's teachings were the Four Noble Truths: 1) all life is suffering, 2) suffering is caused by craving, and therefore, 3) one is able to overcoming suffering by eliminating craving."[36]

"Yes, Buddhism is all about eliminating desires and reaching enlightenment. What has that got to do with abortion?" Baal demanded.

"Only that, as Christopher Kaczor writes, 'If a human being achieved this goal, then this human being would have achieved Nirvana from a Buddhist perspective, but from Boonin's perspective would thereby no longer have a right to life since such a human being, the Buddhist Master, would not have a desire for the future.'"[37]

"Boonin would likely say we should respect his ideal desires or the desires he'd have if he were not a Buddhist monk," said Baal.

"Right, but then it's still not about whether he has the capacity for desires. It's about the type of being he is, the type who should desire a right to life." Feeling satisfied, Amy made a shooing gesture. "It's late. I want to go to bed. And no offense, Baal, but your voice carries. Come back another time."

"Very well," said Baal. "Next time, I would like to discuss Boonin's other book on abortion with you. It's all about the bodily autonomy argument."

35. Beckwith, *Defending Life*, 148

36. Corduan and McCoy, "Buddhism," 125.

37. Kaczor, *Ethics of Abortion*, loc. 67.

"I'll be ready," Chris said, and Baal vanished.

The World's Tiniest Violin Player

It had been a week since Baal's last visit. Chris's buddy Zac was over and they were playing video games.

"Wait, so you'd never heard of David Boonin before, right?" asked Zac.

"Sure," said Chris as he took the fighter on his screen into a nose dive toward an enemy ship.

"Then, how did you know to use his arguments about dead people?" Zac returned.

"Oh, I guess I forgot to mention," Chris said. "I downloaded a few of his books during the conversation and came across it. Anyway, next time he shows up, we're supposed to talk about Boonin's book *Beyond Roe.*"

At that moment, there was a thunder crash and Baal appeared above them. "Hello, Apologetics Man. Are you ready to discuss *Beyond Roe*?"

Zac looked at Chris. "You're right. Everything he says sounds condescending."

Chris smirked. "Yes, I am, Baal. Okay, so what is Boonin's main point in *Beyond Roe*?"

"Boonin is building on Judith Jarvis Thomson's violinist argument.[38] He wants to show that you can be a person with a right to life and still not have the right to use another person's body without their consent. To do this, he tells the real story of Robert McFall and David Shimp. McFall was an asbestos worker who was diagnosed with aplastic anemia. If he was going to survive, he needed a bone marrow transplant. Tests were done for compatibility and the results revealed that his cousin, Shimp, was a match. However, Shimp ended up refusing to undergo further tests, and he said that

38. Thomson, "Defense of Abortion," 332–40.

even if he was completely compatible with McFall, he would not give up his bone marrow."[39]

"Well, that's a pretty lousy move on his part," said Zac.

"Sure, we can agree he was being pretty selfish," Baal shrugged. "McFall clearly agreed because he took his cousin to court and tried to sue him for his bone marrow. Despite Shimp's selfishness however, the presiding judge John P. Flaherty sided with Shimp over McFall.[40] His reasoning was that 'for a society which respects the rights of one individual, to sink it's teeth into the jugular vein or neck of one of its members and suck from it sustenance for another member, is revolting to our hard wrought concepts of jurisprudence.'[41] Sadly, fourteen days later, McFall died.[42] What I get from his decision is this: the law courts have no rights to force you to use your own body to care for someone else. That would be like we are literally feeding on the person. Now, do you both think that Judge Flaherty made the right decision in that case?"

"Yes," Chris and Zac said in unison.

"Excellent, then this is the lesson you should take from it. The state could not force Shimp to give McFall his bone marrow because McFall did not have a right to Shimp's bone marrow. This is true even though McFall was a person with a right to life. If you're ready to accept that, then you should be willing to accept that none of us have a right to use another person's bone marrow even if we need it. Being persons with a right to life can't change that. This can be extended even further. Being a person with a right to life does not give you the right to use another person's body, even if you need it. You need the person's consent. The application to pregnancy, then, is simple. The fetus may be a person with a right to life. But that does not give them a right to use the woman's body. She needs to consent for that.[43] Now, I'm sure you've already thought of objections, so let's hear them."

39. Boonin, *Beyond Roe*, loc. 3.
40. Boonin, *Beyond Roe*, loc. 3.
41. Boonin, *Beyond Roe*, loc. 3.
42. Boonin, *Beyond Roe*, loc. 3.
43. Boonin, *Beyond Roe*, loc. 7–9.

Take Some Responsibility!

"Well, my main objection is to the principle that parents are only obligated to assist their child if they first consent to it," said Chris. "Instead, along with Scott Klusendorf, I contend that women's obligation to their children arise from the fact that they 'willingly engage in an act that is ordered toward procreation.'"[44]

"Why is that significant?" Baal inquired.

"Because as Lee explains, 'The parents first cause the child to be and to be in a dependent and imperiled condition, and then perform an action that kills the child.'[45] Beckwith reasons that if we can hold the parents responsible for caring for born children when they didn't intend for sex to lead to procreation, then it follows that we can hold the pregnant woman responsible as well."[46]

"I think I remember reading a story in one of Canadian Philosopher Paul Chamberlain's books that would apply here," Zac spoke up. "He wrote about Amy Grossberg and Brian Peterson, 'teenage sweethearts, who left a school dance to check into a motel room. There, they delivered their baby boy and threw him into a trash can, where he was left to die. Later, the two went to court for this action, were found guilty of manslaughter, and received jail terms. In addition, they faced the condemnation of the national media and the nation at large, and received a harsh lecture from the judge. "There's a disturbing aspect to your character," he sternly declared, "an egocentrism . . . that blinded you to the intrinsic value of the life of your child."'[47] The pro-choicer can't turn around and say that it was because the newborn baby was a person. They've already granted that the unborn are persons for the sake of the argument. Furthermore, they can't say that it is because the parents consented to being parents. The fact that they threw their baby in the trash can shows that is not the case."

44. Klusendorf, *Case for Life*, 304.

45. Lee, *Abortion and Unborn Human Life*, loc. 137.

46. Beckwith, "Defending Abortion Philosophically," 245.

47. Chamberlain, *Talking About Good and Bad*, 45.

"So, what, responsibilities are generated merely by a biological relationship?" Baal sneered.[48]

"If the idea of responsibility based on biology sounds strange to people, it's only because they've bought into a social contract theory that says obligations only arise from consent. But that's simply not true. As Pearcey writes, 'We also acquire responsibilities to those we are biologically connected to—not only our children but also our parents, brothers, sisters and grandparents.'[49] For example, when you are a child, a parent does not care whether you consent to their rules or not. They expect you to obey them. We are also expected not to kill our siblings, even if we might want to. All that seems left to base obligation on in those instances is the biological connection. So, for Brian and Amy, it could be the biological connection and the fact that they engaged in the act of sexual intercourse at one point, fully aware that it could lead to the creation of a dependent human being."[50]

"This also isn't an uncommon way of speaking of moral obligations. We often hold people accountable for voluntary actions that resulted in consequences that they didn't intend. A drunk driver may not intend to kill another family, but if he does, then he will go to jail for it," Zac pointed out.[51] "Beckwith concludes, 'Such special obligations are . . . necessary in any civilized culture in order to preserve the rights of the vulnerable, the weak, and the young, who can offer very little in exchange for the rights bestowed upon them by the strong and powerful.'[52] It's hard to think of anyone who is more vulnerable, weak, and young than the unborn. So, it is necessary for parents to have special obligations to protect them as well."

48. Boonin, *Defense of Abortion*, 234.
49. Pearcey, *Love Thy Body*, 239.
50. Beckwith, "Defending Abortion Philosophically," 247.
51. Beckwith, "Defending Abortion Philosophically," 247.
52. Beckwith, "Defending Abortion Philosophically," 247.

A Rebuttal to the Responsibility Argument

"Boonin is definitely aware of such an argument. And he has a response!" Baal announced. "He begins by making a distinction between two ways you can be responsible for someone needing your assistance. 1) You can be responsible for the fact that they exist which later causes them to need your help. 2) You can be responsible for making them needy. Boonin argues that if you are responsible in the second sense, then you are obligated to help the person. If you are responsible the first way, you are not. The pregnant woman, he contends is responsible in the first way but not the second, and thus, she is not obligated to assist the unborn child. She only brought him into existence. She did not cause his needy condition. Being needy is a normal part of the unborn's development at that stage. Therefore, there is nothing wrong with her having an abortion."[53]

"How does he come to the conclusion that a person would not be obligated to assist someone if they were only responsible in the first sense?" Chris asked.

"Well, let's go back to the story of McFall and Shimp. Let's imagine that they work together in a lab with toxic chemicals. Shimp gets some on his hands just before he notices McFall is choking. He doesn't have time to wipe them off before running to McFall and giving him the Heimlich maneuver. He does this knowing that his actions could cause McFall to come down with aplastic anemia in the future, and that he has the right bone marrow for a transplant, if necessary. In this case, Shimp would be responsible for McFall's existence. But if McFall were to come down with aplastic anemia, Boonin is sure that none of us would argue that Shimp is required to give him his bone marrow."[54]

"That's an interesting response," Chris conceded. "And I actually find myself in agreement with Boonin. Shimp would still not be required to give McFall his bone marrow in that situation. In fact, I would go even farther and say that even if Shimp was

53. Boonin, *Beyond Roe*, loc. 74–75, 79–80.

54. Boonin, *Beyond Roe*, 82.

responsible for making McFall needy, he shouldn't be expected to give him bone marrow."

Baal rocked back on his heels. "I would not expect that from you. Wouldn't it be incredibly selfish for Shimp not to help someone he had made worse off?"

"Sure, but there are other ways he could help, such as financial compensation," Chris replied. "The big issue in Boonin's book is that he never quite grasps the reason why pro-lifers don't believe McFall has a right to Shimp's bone marrow. I would argue that to force Shimp to give McFall his bone marrow would be extraordinary and wholly unethical behavior because it is not natural for us to give up our bone marrow to someone else." Baal started to open his mouth to object but Chris rushed to say, "That doesn't apply to a pregnant woman! A woman's womb is designed to gestate a fetus. It is not an unnatural, extraordinary act at all."[55]

"Boonin does have a response to that kind of argument in chapter 17 of his book," Baal replied. "But that would get us off the topic of the responsibility argument. Can we table that for now?"[56]

"Yes, that's fine. If Boonin is right and the woman has no responsibility for the fetus, then the proper function of her uterus is a moot point," Chris agreed.

"Okay, so I'm assuming that you still believe that the woman is responsible for the kid's neediness and that she is obligated to assist him?" Baal asked.

"That's right and for a couple of reasons," Chris nodded. "First, I'm not convinced that the reasons that Shimp has no special obligation to McFall would apply to the pregnant woman.

55. This is a modified version of a point that Nash makes in *The Abolition of Women*, 176. She is talking about the violinist argument vs. pregnancy. You will find that many of the rebuttals to the violinist argument cross over pretty easily to the Robert McFall and David Shimp story.

56. I have written a whole series of articles reviewing *Beyond Roe*. I review Boonin's rebuttals to that and the parental responsibility argument in Christiansen, "Persons of Interest." While Boonin's rebuttal to the responsibility argument could still make it morally permissible for a woman to have an abortion, it abandons the presupposition that the violinist argument seems to rest on, namely, that remaining pregnant goes above and beyond what we expect of parents.

Shimp still did not bring McFall into being or make him needy but, in a brave act, extended his life with the Heimlich maneuver. The act of extending McFall's life with the result that he later developed aplastic anemia and needed a bone marrow transplant is quite different from conceiving a child. When parents have sex and conceive a child, they both bring him into existence *and* cause him to be needy. So, they are responsible in the sense that Boonin says would obligate them to assist their child."[57]

"Are you denying his point that the baby needs the mother's womb because of his or her stage of development?" Baal pushed.

"No. I'm saying that there is significance in the fact that, as Kate Greasley writes, 'The fetus's biological inability to survive outside the womb is true of all early human life,' whereas the condition of choking that threatened McFall was an extraordinary ailment.[58] She goes onto to say that 'what is ordinarily requited for human beings to remain alive does not usually suffice as an explanation for death.'"[59]

"Otherwise, defense attorneys could have a hay day," Zac chimed in. He stood up and struck the pose of a lawyer making a case. "'Your honor, my client did not kill this man by shooting him. What killed him was that his body never developed in a way that could survive a bullet passing through it.' The judge would probably laugh that lawyer out of court."[60]

"Or consider Patrick Lee's story about a motorboating accident," Chris added. "'Suppose I am in a motorboat in a lake and, speeding past the pier, I knock three or four children into the lake.'[61] Would you and Boonin agree that I am responsible for them now being in need of assistance?"

57. Lee, *Abortion and Unborn Human Life*, loc. 122.

58. Greasley, *Arguments About Abortion*, 50. Greasley's book is another essential read for pro-lifers. She also gives a cogent argument for how abortion is an act of killing and not simply letting die. She lays out some of the abortion procedures which pro-lifers can quote. And she shows that even letting someone die can be an act of killing.

59. Greasley, *Arguments About Abortion*, 50.

60. This is based off of Greasley, *Arguments About Abortion*, 50.

61. Lee, *Abortion and Unborn Human Life*, loc. 122.

"If they can't swim, certainly," Baal nodded.

"So, I should go back and pull them out of the water before they drown?"

"Yes."

"Well, I disagree based on the principles that Boonin has laid out. Lee goes on to write, 'I might also claim that I was only responsible for their being in the water, not for their being in an imperiled condition. It is not my fault . . . that they do not know how to swim, and so their dependency condition is a consequence of what I do, not something I'm responsible for.'[62] Do you think that is an excuse that anyone would accept?"

"Well, I might. Children are noisy, smelly, and expensive. But you humans are lot more sentimental. So, Boonin and others would likely be horrified by such a suggestion," Baal sighed.

"Great. Then, as Lee concludes, 'Clearly, it is specious to distinguish between my causing them to be in the water . . . and their being in a dependency condition due to their inability to swim. . . . But, likewise, it is specious to distinguish between a child's existing . . . and his existing in an imperiled condition,'"[63] Chris concluded.

"So, I think that shows that Boonin is wrong about the parents not being responsible in a way that obligates them to help. And his reasons for saying that the parents are not responsible for a fetus's neediness lead us to absurdities that even he couldn't accept," Zac summed up. "And just to bring the conversation full circle, his distinction would leave us no way to condemn what Amy and Brian did to their newborn baby."

"I've been thinking a little about that!" Baal announced. "And I think that we can condemn them."

"I'm listening," Zac leaned forward with interest.

"He changes the story of McFall and Shimp so that, in this version, Shimp agrees to let McFall have his bone marrow. They go through the whole nine months plugged into each other and McFall lives. However, six months later, Shimp decides that he regrets

62. Lee, *Abortion and Unborn Human Life*, loc.122.

63. Lee, *Abortion and Unborn Human Life*, loc. 122–23.

giving McFall his bone marrow and decides to shoot him. Now, do you think that this would be right of Shimp to do?"[64]

"No, that would certainly be immoral and illegal," said Chris.

"Great. Now, remember the lesson that Boonin says we're allowed to draw from Mcfall and Shimp. The lesson is that Shimp has a right to decide not to let McFall use his body. It is not that Shimp should have a right to kill McFall after he doesn't need to use to his body anymore. In the same way, a woman has a right to decide to not let a fetus use her body. But she does not have a right to kill him after he doesn't need her body anymore."[65]

"Boonin is using incredibly misleading terminology, though," said Zac. "He says the lesson is that the pregnant woman should be allowed to stop a baby from using her body. But the method he is saying she should be allowed to use is abortion. And abortion certainly kills the baby. Look at Greasley's descriptions of the most common method:

> *Vacuum aspiration or suction termination:* . . . The cervix of the pregnant woman is stretched open and the surgeon inserts a plastic tube into the womb. The surgeon then uses a suction tube to evacuate the contents of the womb, in the process of which the fetus is dismembered by the vacuum machine.[66]

"When living human beings are dismembered, they are killed."

"If your problem is that the procedures directly kill the child, a woman could always have a hysterotomy or hysterectomy. In those, the baby is simply removed from the womb and left to die," Baal suggested.[67]

"Except that you can kill someone even if you don't directly attack their bodies," Zac returned. "For example, if a nurse turns off all the life support units in an intensive care ward, then she has

64. Boonin, *Beyond Roe*, 50.
65. Boonin, *Beyond Roe*, 50–51.
66. Greasley, *Arguments About Abortion*, 47.
67. Greasley, *Arguments About Abortion*, 48.

surely killed the patients rather than simply allowed them to die, as Greasley points out."[68]

"What makes the difference, do you think?" Baal pressed.

"Again, it comes down to the fact that she is responsible for caring for them," Zac replied.

"There's a second misleading statement," Chris went on. "Boonin says that the lesson of Shimp and McFall does not entail us to say that a woman can kill her child after he no longer needs to use her body. But that gives the impression that a child at six months old does not need his mother's body to survive anymore. I'm not a baby expert, but I'm pretty sure that they are still heavily dependent on their parents' bodies."

"I have a kid and another one on the way," Zac raised a hand. "I can testify to the fact that they still need someone to feed them, clothe them, and clean up after them when they've made a mess."

"And Boonin even talks about how he has a kid in the passage you quoted to me when we first started talking!" Chris reminded Baal. "He should know this better than anyone. So, let's put this all together. A mother has a right to kill her child to stop him from using her body. And six-month-old children do not stop using their mother's body once they are born. This gives us everything we need to justify infanticide. On this model, all a mother would have to do to be justified in killing her baby is to stop consenting to letting him or her use her body."

"And, of course, we can apply this to the case of Brian and Amy," Zac added. "Their son was newly born, so he was even more dependent than a six-month-old. Their son did not have a right to use their bodies, even though he needed them to survive without their consent. Amy and Brian didn't consent. So, he had no right to use their bodies. And therefore, there should have been nothing wrong with leaving him to die in a hotel garbage bin." Zac shuddered. "I feel dirty just saying that."

"It's funny, but we're talking about abandoning babies alive in trash bins like it's a future possibility," Chris mused. In actuality, it's a reality. Jonathon Van Maren interviewed a Canadian nurse who

68. Greasley, *Arguments About Abortion*, 49.

talked about a live birth she witnessed and '*the doctor hastily tossing the tiny child into a trash can, where she heard the baby rustling weakly among the papers before he died.*'[69] I really don't see much of a difference between what happened at that clinic and what Amy and Brian did, other than that there's no mention of the doctor going to jail for it."

"A lot of these arguments seem very familiar to me," Baal muttered.

"They ought to," Chris replied. "They are all responses that pro-life apologists made to Boonin when he made the exact same arguments in *A Defense of Abortion*. Tell me, does he reference any pro-life authors in *Beyond Roe*?"

"He mentions some in the conclusion as suggestions for further reading. But not in the main body of the book," Baal admitted.

"That's a shame. Otherwise, he could have actually engaged with the rebuttals and potentially avoided the same mistakes in logic that he'd made previously," Chris shrugged.

Conclusion

"So, it doesn't sound like you are overly impressed with Boonin's books," Baal sighed.

"I fully admit that he made a valiant effort to meet pro-lifers halfway in *A Defense of Abortion*," Chris assured him. "The problem was that he often seems to misunderstand what pro-life arguments are and thus doesn't truly engage with them. And his own criteria for what grounds human rights lead to absurd conclusions that even he cannot accept. So, he ends up falling back on the same criteria that pro-life people are using."

"And as for *Beyond Roe*," Zac added, "he failed to pick a situation that was truly analogous to pregnancy. Even worse, he leaves the door open for child abandonment and infanticide. And his arguments against our position still have all the same problems."

69. Van Maren, *Culture War*, 120.

"By the way, I still haven't forgotten that you're a demon," Chris narrowed his eyes. "Should I exorcise you, or will you see yourself out?"

"Don't bother. I don't want to waste my time further. Goodbye!" Baal vanished in a puff of smoke.

"Huh, I guess even he couldn't . . . 'Baal' Boonin's arguments out," Chris laughed

Zac rolled his eyes. "You're sick."

Bibliography

Alleyne, Blaise, and Jonathon Van Maren. *A Guide to Discussing Assisted Suicide*. Toronto: Life Cycle, 2017.

Arnold, Bill T., and Bryan E. Beyer. *Readings from the Ancient Near East: Primary Sources for Old Testament Study*. Grand Rapids: Baker Academic, 2002.

Beckwith, Francis J. "Defending Abortion Philosophically: A Review of David Boonin's *A Defense of Abortion*." *Journal of Medicine and Philosophy* 31 (2006) 177–203.

———. *Defending Life: A Moral and Legal Case Against Abortion Choice*. Cambridge: Cambridge University Press, 2007.

Benatar, David. *Better Never to Have Been: The Harm of Coming into Existence*. Oxford: Oxford University Press, 2006. Kindle ed.

Boonin, David. *Beyond Roe: Why Abortion Should Be Legal—Even If the Fetus Is a Person*. Oxford: Oxford University Press, 2019. Kindle ed.

———. *Dead Wrong: The Ethics of Posthumous Harm*. Oxford: Oxford University Press, 2019. Kindle ed.

———. *A Defense of Abortion*. Cambridge: Cambridge University Press, 2003.

Brock, Dan W. "Cloning Human Beings: An Assessment of the Ethical Issues Pro and Con." Georgetown University Bioethics Archive, E3-E-24. https://bioethicsarchive.georgetown.edu/nbac/pubs/cloning2/cc5.pdf.

Chamberlain, Paul. *Can We Be Good Without God? A Conversation About Truth, Morality, Culture, and a Few Other Things That Matter*. Downers Grove: InterVarsity, 1996.

———. "A Case Against Physician Assisted Suicide." Ch. 19 in *Do the Right Thing: Readings in Applied Ethics and Social Philosophy*, edited by Francis J. Beckwith. Belmont, CA: Wadsworth, 1996. http://www.monge.net/phil7mm/coursedocs/Chamberlain.pdf.

———. *Final Wishes: A Cautionary Tale on Death, Dignity, and Physician Assisted Suicide*. Eugene, OR: Wipf & Stock, 2000.

———. *Talking About Good and Bad Without Getting Ugly: A Guide to Moral Persuasion*. Downers Grove: InterVarsity, 2005.

———. *Why People Don't Believe: Confronting Seven Challenges to the Christian Faith.* Grand Rapids: Baker, 2011.

Christiansen, Chris. "Persons of Interest: A Review of David Boonin's *Beyond Roe*, Part 4." Human Defense Initiative, July 3, 2022. https://humandefense.com/persons-of-interest-a-response-to-david-boonins-beyond-roe-part-4/.

College of Pharmacists of British Columbia. "New Federal Legislation Brings Changes to MAID Eligibility, Safeguards, and Monitoring." BC Pharmacists, March 22, 2021. https://www.bcpharmacists.org/news/new-federal-legislation-brings-changes-maid-eligibility-safeguards-and-monitoring?fbclid=IwAR0A4-f6B2PuXR0T8TrZKDY18di_svwoS6FE4cqMr_F6QsDW070pVhthhJI.

Connors, Stephanie Gray. *Start with What: 10 Principles for Thinking About Physician Assisted Suicide.* N.p., FL: Wongeese, 2020. Kindle ed.

Copan, Paul. *Is God a Moral Monster? Making Sense of the Old Testament God.* Grand Rapids: Baker, 2011. Kindle ed.

Corduan, Winfried, and Daniel McCoy. "Buddhism." In *The Popular Handbook of World Religions*, edited by Daniel McCoy, 123–38. Eugene, OR: Harvest House, 2021.

Darth Yucko. "She Stole His Sign and Got Arrested." YouTube video, 4:24, May 16, 2019. https://www.youtube.com/watch?v=cDI9QRzPzec&t=3s.

Davis, John Jefferson. *Evangelical Ethics: Issues Facing the Church Today.* 3rd ed. Phillipsburg, PA: P&R, 2004.

Dawkins, Richard. *The God Delusion.* Boston: Houghton Mifflin, 2008.

Disability Link. "What Is Not Dead Yet of GA About?" https://disabilitylink.org/not-dead-yet/.

George, Robert P., and Patrick Lee. "Acorns and Embryos: On Bad Metaphors in the Debate About the Beginning of Life." *New Atlantis* 7 (Fall 2004–Winter 2005) 90–100. https://www.thenewatlantis.com/publications/acorns-and-embryos.

George, Robert P., and Christopher Tollefsen. *Embryo: A Defense of Human Life.* Princeton, NJ: Witherspoon Institute, 2011. Kindle ed.

Gray, Stephanie. *Love Unleashes Life: Abortion and the Art of Communicating Truth.* Toronto: Life Cycle, 2015.

Greasley, Kate. *Arguments About Abortion: Personhood, Morality and Law.* Oxford: Oxford University Press, 2017.

Harvard Right to Life. "Peter Singer and Stephanie Gray Connors Debate, 'Resolved: Abortion is Immoral.'" Youtube video, 1:29:08, Oct. 31, 2020. https://www.youtube.com/watch?v=DB5IZXGmko8&t=2432s.

Horn, Trent. *Persuasive Pro-Life: How to Talk About Our Culture's Toughest Issue.* El Cajun, CA: Catholic Answers, 2014.

Johnson, Craig E. *Meeting the Ethical Challenges of Leadership: Casting Light or Shadow.* Los Angeles: Sage, 2021.

Kaczor, Christopher. *Disputes in Bioethics: Abortion, Euthanasia, and Other Controversies.* Notre Dame: University of Notre Dame, 2020. Kindle ed.

———. *The Ethics of Abortion: Women's Rights, Human Life, and the Question of Justice*. New York: Routledge, 2015.

Kathryn. "Loved Too Late." Silent No More Awareness. https://www.silentnomoreawareness.org/testimonies/testimony.aspx?ID=3471.

King, Martin Luther, Jr. "Letter from a Birmingham Jail." In *Readings in Moral Philosophy*, edited by Jonathan Wolff, 522–30. New York: Norton, 2018.

Klusendorf, Scott. *The Case for Life: Equipping Christians to Engage the Culture*. Wheaton, IL: Crossway, 2009.

Koukl, Greg. *Tactics: A Game Plan for Discussing your Christian Convictions*. 10th anniversary ed. Grand Rapids: Zondervan, 2019. Kindle ed.

Lee, Patrick. *Abortion and Unborn Human Life*. 2nd ed. Washington, DC: Catholic University of America Press, 2010.

Lewis, C. S. *The Abolition of* Man. New York: HarperOne, 1975.

———. "Dogma and the Universe." In *God in the Dock*, 24–35. Grand Rapids: Eerdmans, 1970.

LutheranSatire. "Horus Reads the Internet." YouTube video, 6:13, Oct. 19, 2014. https://www.youtube.com/watch?v=4r2m_cffRjI.

McMahan, Jeff. *The Ethics of Killing: Problems at the Margins of Life*. Oxford: Oxford University Press, 2002. Kindle ed.

Nash, Fiorella. *The Abolition of Woman: How Radical Feminism Is Betraying Women*. San Francisco: Ignatius, 2018.

Newman, Marc. *Contenders: A Church Wide Strategy to Unmask Abortion, Defeat Its Advocates, Empower Christians, and Change the World*. Sevierville, TN: Refocus, 2020. Kindle ed.

Newport, John P. *The New Age Movement and the Biblical Worldview: Conflict and Dialogue*. Grand Rapids: Eerdmans, 1998.

Pearcey, Nancy R. *Love Thy Body: Answering Hard Questions About Life and Sexuality*. Grand Rapids: Baker, 2018.

Peyton, Laura. "Supreme Court Says Yes to Doctor Assisted Suicide in Specific Cases." Canadian Broacasting Company, Feb. 6, 2015. https://www.cbc.ca/news/politics/supreme-court-says-yes-to-doctor-assisted-suicide-in-specific-cases-1.2947487.

Rae, Scott B. *Introducing Christian Ethics: A Short Guide to Making Moral Choices*. Grand Rapids: Zondervan, 2016.

Rawls, John. *Political Liberalism*. New York: Columbia University Press, 2005.

Royal BC Museum. "Orcas: Our Shared Future." https://royalbcmuseum.bc.ca/visit/exhibitions/orcas-our-shared-future.

Singer, Peter. "All Animals Are Equal." In *Readings in Moral Philosophy*, edited by Jonathan Wolff, 429–35. New York: Norton, 2018. Kindle ed.

———. *Ethics in the Real World: 90 Essays on Things that Matter*. Princeton: Princeton University Press, 2023.

———. *Practical Ethics*. 3rd ed. Cambridge: Cambridge University Press, 2011.

Spielberg, Steven, dir. *Jurassic Park*. Universal City, CA: Universal Studios, 1993.

Stackhouse, John G. *Making the Best of It: Following Christ in the Real World*. Oxford: Oxford University Press, 2008.

Stirton, Ruth, and David Lawrence. "No Pain, All Gain: The Case for Farming Organs in Brainless Humans." *Journal of Medical Ethics* Forum (blog), June 10, 2017. https://blogs.bmj.com/medical-ethics/2017/06/10/no-pain-all-gain-the-case-for-farming-organs-in-brainless-humans/.

Sue. "Sue's 2023 March for Life Testimony." Silent No More Awareness. https://www.silentnomoreawareness.org/testimonies/testimony.aspx?ID=4117.

Tarico, Valerie. "Why I Am Pro-Abortion, Not Just Pro Choice." *Free Inquiry* 36.5 (2016). https://secularhumanism.org/2016/07/cont-why-i-am-pro-abortion-not-just-pro-choice/.

Thompson, David G. "The High Price of Unity: The Universal Declaration of Human Rights." In *Everyday Theology: How to Read Cultural Texts and Interpret Trends*, edited by Kevin J. Vanhoozer et al., 99–113. Grand Rapids: Baker Academic, 2007.

Thomson, Judith Jarvis. "A Defense of Abortion." In *Readings in Moral Philosophy*, edited by Jonathan Wolff, 332–40. New York: Norton, 2018.

Tooley, Michael. "Abortion and Infanticide." *Philosophy and Public Affairs* 2.1 (1972) 37–65.

Toronto Sun. "Caught on Camera: Man Kicked Woman at Anti-Abortion Rally." YouTube video, 0:37, Oct. 5, 2018. https://www.youtube.com/watch?v=oImcOC9jRqs.

United Nations. "Convention on the Rights of the Child." Nov. 20, 1989. https://www.ohchr.org/en/instruments-mechanisms/instruments/convention-rights-child.

———. "Universal Declaration of Human Rights." https://www.un.org/en/about-us/universal-declaration-of-human-rights.

van der Breggen, Hendrik. *Untangling Popular Pro-Choice Arguments: Critical Thinking About Abortion*. N.p.: Amazon KDP, 2018. Kindle ed.

Van Maren, Jonathon. *The Culture War.* Toronto: Life Cycle, 2016.

———. *Seeing Is Believing: Why Our Culture Must Face the Victims of Abortion*. Toronto: Life Cycle, 2018.

Warnock, Mary, and Elisabeth MacDonald. *Easeful Death: Is There a Case for Assisted Dying?* Oxford: Oxford University Press, 2008.

Warren, Mary Anne. "On the Moral and Legal Status of Abortion." In *Morality and Moral Controversies: Readings in Moral, Social, and Political Philosophy*, edited by Steven Scalet and John Arthur, 342–50. New York: Routledge, 2019.

Wolff, Jonathan. *An Introduction to Moral Philosophy.* New York: Norton, 2018.

———. *Readings in Moral Philosophy*. New York: Norton, 2018.

World Health Organization. "Palliative Care." Aug. 5, 2020. https://www.who.int/news-room/fact-sheets/detail/palliative-care.

WSYX ABC 6. "Caught on Camera: Pro-Life Activist Confronted and Attacked by Woman." YouTube video, 2:55, July 10, 2014. https://www.youtube.com/watch?v=vCJf9boyB5Y.

www.ingramcontent.com/pod-product-compliance
Lightning Source LLC
LaVergne TN
LVHW020652100826
845148LV00012B/2449

* 9 7 9 8 3 8 5 2 5 9 9 1 5 *